SUCCESSFUL MANAGEMENT

Successful Management

Neville Bain

Foreword by Sir Adrian Cadbury

First published 1995 by
MACMILLAN PRESS LTD
Houndmills, Basingstoke, Hampshire RG21 6XS
and London
Companies and representatives
throughout the world

ISBN 0–333–64347–X

A catalogue record for this book is available
from the British Library.

10   9   8   7   6   5   4   3   2   1
04   03   02   01   00   99   98   97   96   95

Copy-edited and typeset by Povey–Edmondson
Okehampton and Rochdale, England

Printed and bound in Great Britain by
Mackays of Chatham PLC, Chatham, Kent

Families provide support, perspective and rich learning experiences – mine more than most! This book is especially for **Anni**, as well as for **Sue**, **Peter** and **Kristina**.

Contents

List of Case Studies and Figures

Case studies

Figures

Foreword

Neville Bain's book fills an unquestioned gap in management literature and that is a rare accolade! His guide to successful management is grounded in experience, practical in its approach and blessedly free from jargon.

Having worked closely with Neville, it will come as no surprise that I wholeheartedly support his analysis and conclusions. His advice on how to get the best out of consultants, on the power of teams and on the need for a sense of balance will prove invaluable to those taking up their first major post as a general manager.

I particularly appreciated the strategic theme which, along with the theme of change, runs through the book. Neville stresses the need to establish a clear strategy from the outset; clear not only to its author – 'strategy is the creature of the business leader' – but to everyone on whose efforts its successful implementation depends. *Successful Management* contains as helpful an account as I have read of how to formulate a strategy which can adapt to rapid changes in the competitive environment.

Turning strategy into action depends on leadership and on the calibre and commitment of those who make up the enterprise. I entirely agree with Neville's comment that 'Managers continue to underestimate the intelligence and latent ability of the workforce to contribute to strategy execution.' As he goes on to say, 'The workforce remains a significant source of untapped value.' It is one which is drawn on to gain a competitive advantage by the best of our overseas competitors.

It follows that I fully endorse Neville's emphasis on the necessity for managers and directors to devote time to their own training and development. We expect it of those for whom we are responsible and they have every right to expect it of us. The way to bring about a positive attitude to training is to ensure that those managers who train and bring on their successors are seen to be rewarded for so doing. Who gains in the pay and promotion stakes is an indication of where the priorities of a company really lie. On appointments, I like his advice to promote, if anything, a shade too soon; this is the safest kind of risk to take.

The lesson I draw from reading this authoritative work is that there can be no let up for any of us in the drive to become more professional and more effective as managers. 'But then', as Neville says, 'Whoever wanted a quiet life?'

SIR ADRIAN CADBURY

Preface

The aim of this book is to provide managers with a practical guide that will help them to be more successful. Far too often, preparation is left to chance and a new incumbent is left to his or her own devices to settle into a new management position. Today, a number of management candidates will have had the advantage of a business school education which will provide a practical base of methodology. However, many of the business schools rely heavily on systematic techniques which certainly clarify the mind but all too frequently seem to be difficult to apply in the real world. There is, I believe, scope for a very practical guide of approaches which have worked well in practice and can be examined for relevance in the particular setting of the reader. Within this framework, references are made to appropriate literature to provide a richer range of views on the chosen topics.

This book does not try to replicate the scope of an MBA programme. However, it will provide helpful, additional insights to the MBA and other business and management students on MBA, post-experience and executive courses. The approach is to demonstrate practically how theory in action can lead to successful management. I hope a wide audience from business will be attracted to this work because of the broad scope covered. Managers in today's and tomorrow's business setting will increasingly need to have a broader grasp of general management principles. Those entering management for the first time should find this book helpful, practical and topical.

Every manager operating in a commercial environment needs to remember that their prime role is to create wealth for the shareholders. They need to understand clearly the fundamental links with shareholder value as measured by the capital market and the financial and strategic performance of the company and its component parts. This means that managers need to set the right objectives for the company in which they have that responsibility. They certainly need clear objectives for themselves. To set priorities, managers must first have clearly understood the nature of the task of value creation. A general manager must develop new strategies that are relevant to the environment and are based on the core competences of the corporation. These strategies will need to yield a long-term competitive advantage so that they significantly increase the value of the company over time. This, then, is the most basic framework or the central proposition. This message is therefore repeated in different forms through the book. While strategy creation is the primary responsibility of the general manager, the wider group of management will have participated in the process and will certainly be responsible for a part of the execution. It is therefore of wide interest to the total management population.

Supporting this core thesis there are four recurring themes in this book:

1. *A fast-changing environment* is the regular background against which managers must manage. Change is continuous and will be more rapid as we move forward over time. The organisation must be capable of reacting to those changes and taking advantage of them yet staying within the overall framework of the agreed corporate strategy.
2. *The role of strategy* is fundamental if the people in the organisation are to be enabled to make the contribution of which they are capable. Strategy based on a good grasp of the core competences of a business is an essential precursor to achieving optimal shareholder value.
3. *Dependence on people* is key to delivering the latent capability of a business. People are the greatest source of competitive advantage which is the primary reason why we should invest in their capability.
4. While *the concept of leadership* is less easy to prescribe, it is an important attribute which must be present in all successful general managers. It is certainly not an asset one is born with, rather it is a skill that can be honed by practice.

The genesis of the book lies with the notion that most general managers with whom I spoke had very little help in preparation for general management. In most cases they were 'thrown in at the deep end', surviving or sinking depending on their intuitive reactions, and their skills were built up over time. It was this thought, coupled with the lack of a systematic approach to identifying potential general managers that prompted a survey of not only senior general managers but also of professionals expert in recruiting to gain deeper insight into factors regarded as important for success in management. While this survey dwelt particularly on the appointment for the first time to a general management role, it was clear from follow-up discussions that this same malaise was apparent at other levels of management. The simple fact that emerges is that although many senior managers understand that people can be a great source of added value, in practice too little attention is paid to skill development. Chapter 1 begins with the survey, setting down principles and questions that are addressed in more depth later.

The book is organised topically so that the reader can dip into areas of interest in whatever order preferred. However the opening chapter is best read first, because it sets the scene and makes some initial observations that can be tested in later chapters. The next two chapters, Management or Leadership and Management Development, are universally important whatever the reader's managerial role. Looking outwards is an essential characteristic of a successful general manager. It therefore follows that the chapter on the environment is important for many aspects of management and is best read early.

While there remain those who rely on instinct or hope in their management role, this minority is rapidly being replaced by those who have developed a distinct capability and who constantly brush up on techniques and learn from the experience of others. It is my hope that this book helps in a small way to raise standards through thoughtful consideration of important aspects of successful management.

NEVILLE BAIN

Acknowledgements

I must start with a general but important acknowledgement to the many managers who have influenced this book. Throughout my work career I have been impressed with the very positive attributes of successful managers with whom I have worked or come into contact who have often had diverse backgrounds and different styles. This has provided a great deal of resource for the book as well as positively influencing my own style of management.

Then, more specifically, I appreciate the input of more than 90 managers who provided responses to the questionnaire discussed in Chapter 1 and many of whom provided follow-up information. Some colleagues and former colleagues have made valuable suggestions in specific parts of this work. Russell Walls, formerly Finance Director of Coats Viyella Plc, helped with his suggestions on numbers, while Bill Shardlow, Personnel Director of Coats Viyella Plc, provided suggestions to improve the final draft as well as commenting on a number of the personnel issues raised.

James Watt of The LEK Partnership was generous both in helpful comments and providing some material which has been included. Equally, Bob Cowell of Makinson Cowell provided charts for the chapter on Communication as well as some suggestions for improvement. Louise Charlton of Brunswick also made suggestions on the broad topic of communication which I have been pleased to incorporate. Peter Stafford of Touche Ross helpfully provided information for the case study of the Capital Goods Manufacturer in Chapter 11. Stephen Rutt of Macmillan made many helpful, practical suggestions on the layout and content. I am grateful for his contribution.

Professor David Band, Dean of the Faculty of Business at Leeds Metropolitan University and formerly Director of the Advanced Business Programme at Otago University, was generous with his time and advice, having ploughed through the three drafts in total. His encouragement, warm support and advice is greatly appreciated. Ruth Tait of Korn/Ferry Carré/Orban International also provided encouragement and very helpful suggestions following her appraisal of the second draft.

Sir Adrian Cadbury has been an outstanding role model, mentor and friend during my 27 years with Cadbury Schweppes. He has always been warmly supportive with his encouragement to reach higher goals in business life. His thoughtful suggestions, having read the draft in detail, were greatly appreciated. He also kindly agreed to write the foreword to this book.

Lord Sheppard must have one of the busiest schedules of any businessman that I know! However, he kindly agreed to read the final draft, making numerous useful observations. I very much appreciate his time and advice.

This book has been improved as a result of wider work quoted and where permission has been obtained for inclusion and where acknowledgement is made in the body of the book. I would especially like to thank the following for their permission to use material.

- Pat and Ron Knight of People Change Organisation (PCO) for Figure 2.1.
- *Chief Executive* magazine for permission to include the GE Assessment.
- Simon & Schuster Inc. for permission to use Michael Porter's Five Competitive Forces shown on p. 90 derived from Porter's book, *Competitive Advantage: Creating and Sustaining Superior Performance*.
- Ian Pearson and Peter Cochrane of BT Laboratories for permission to use an abridged version of their 200 Futures for the Year 2020.
- *Fortune*, for Alex Taylor III's insights into General Motors' turn around which was published in *Fortune*, October 17, 1994.

The production of this book would not have been possible without the substantial input of Sue McBain who typed up early roughs and retyped the many corrections and amendments. She struggled with obscure notes as well as difficult handwriting to take the work to its final stage. She was also helped by Patricia Taylor who typed a large part of the first draft.

Many people have helped, guided and encouraged but the resultant work, blemishes and all, is my responsibility. My hope is that this input will have produced a worthwhile book, helpful to a wide audience interested in successful management.

NEVILLE BAIN

1   Starting-Point

Background

The starting-point is a survey which produced seventy responses from successful senior managers and twenty professionals who were working in the field of executive search or who were providing services to firms on selection techniques. The survey was undertaken to establish the following:

- How are general managers chosen and what support are they given early in their first post?
- What were their first significant actions?
- What are the most important characteristics in a general manager, and how are these likely to change in the future?
- How do successful managers divide their time amongst aspects of their jobs, and how does this compare with what the professionals expect?

The survey response rate was over 70 per cent and it was heartening to see the expressions of interest in this general area, as one where managers wanted more information, and where they felt that practical improvements were necessary. In about 25 per cent of the cases there was some follow up with direct discussion or further correspondence.

Although the sample was international including United Kingdom, Europe, the United States of America, Australia, New Zealand, South Africa and India, there were no significant variations between responses, in part because the sample size of individual overseas countries was not large enough.

Most of the managers in the sample were senior general managers, well-qualified with a degree and an MBA or having attended an advanced business programme at a recognised business school. The sample population was older with 52 per cent over 50 years and 33 per cent between 41 and 50 years of age. No one was younger than 31 years.

Broad observations

Very few senior general managers were truly focused on the time frame of five to ten years forward, thinking about the capabilities of managers that

1

would be needed for survival, growth and outperformance in the years ahead. While there is considerable evidence of change around all of us, even managers of the successful firms today were spending only a small amount of time and resource on thinking about the future. Further, the great majority of managers were locked into past performance as the main precursor to future success in the selection of new managers. At best, this must be regarded as a challengeable approach which may not stand the test of time as the success factors for managers of the future will not necessarily be rooted in historical performance.

Developing this further, very few newly appointed managers find real help in the most crucial change of their corporate careers, the change to general management. This was also true earlier in their careers when taking on a new management role. It was out of this blinding flash of the obvious that it became clear that a focus on general management was an important area for observation in an endeavour to significantly uplift management standards. To get started, let us dwell on the messages gleaned from the international survey.

First general management role

Most managers (72 per cent) were appointed to their first general management role internally and of these slightly more than half had received some Business School training prior to their appointment. In a number of cases this was a considerable time before the appointment. As one manager replied 'I received my MBA prior to any significant work experience', and another 'I attended an Advanced Business Programme 4 years prior'.

When these new general managers were appointed to their first role 80 per cent received no training or preparation at all. Some undertook some personal reading but most were left on their own. The few that received some help for the new role did not get very much! 'I was given a book on company director's responsibilities' was one comment, while another observed, 'I had two one-day training events to cover gaps in my knowledge base'. Only 9 per cent of those responding believed that they received good or comprehensive help on taking charge for the first time.

This experience contrasts with expectations of the managers surveyed who felt that it was very desirable to provide formal training prior to a general management appointment. This was the view of almost 90 per cent of respondents. Those who did not place a high value on pre-appointment training observed that training was 'unnecessary if you have done an MBA', and 'Management is an art not a science'. Following up some of the responses there was a feeling amongst some managers that 'experience is a better teacher' so that greater efforts should be made in providing a rich variety of experiences prior to an appointment rather than 'topping up with techniques of questionable value'.

There was a variety of first actions taken by newly appointed managers, which reflected two things. First the needs of the company, as perceived by the new general manager, and second the manager's background which influenced the analysis of the company. In order of frequency the following picture of first actions taken by newly appointed managers emerged from the replies:

Rank		No of mentions
1.	Strategy review	46
2.	Organisational change	27
3.	Listening and learning	25
4.	Business review, improve performance	17
5.	Others	5

(The maximum score was 70 and a number of managers listed two action points.)

Most important attributes of general managers

The questionnaire invited managers to rank attributes in priority order as those considered most important in general managers. It should be made clear that the questionnaire concentrated upon attributes rather than specific management skills. There are very specific skills or competencies that are clearly necessary for any general manager, including for example:

- financial appreciation and judgement;
- Information Technology awareness;
- basics of strategy formulation, development and implementation;
- specialist technical, as distinct from commercial, skills, where they are necessary.

These basic skills are of course crucial and if potential general managers do not possess them, then somebody must identify their aptitude to learn and apply them. There can be no question of making an appointment to general management without these skills being firmly in place, or capable of being absorbed prior to the effective date of the appointment.

The choice offered was:

Ability to communicate
Drive, energy
Intellectual capacity
Interpersonal skills
Knowledge of the industry
Leadership
Successful track record
Others

Those specifying 'others' included judgement, vision, ability to listen, and external awareness.

Managers were clear that the four most important characteristics were, in order:

1. Leadership
2. Drive and energy
3. Ability to communicate
4. Interpersonal skills

It is interesting to compare this with the ranking given by the professionals which was:

1st equal   Leadership and intellectual capacity
2.   Drive, energy
3.   Ability to communicate
4.   Interpersonal skills

This is shown in detail in Figure 1.1.

The major difference is that the professionals valued intellectual capacity more highly than drive and energy, as they could see a need for managers to deal with more complex structures especially in the future, when time pressures would also be more acute. When thinking about the future it was felt by the great majority of professionals that the key characteristics for success would be largely unchanged. Most replied, 'more of the same', but two observed that 'the need to communicate would increase' while another suggested that 'interpersonal skills would become more important'. Managers felt that knowledge of the industry was fifth most important yet this was rated only marginally important by only one of the professionals.

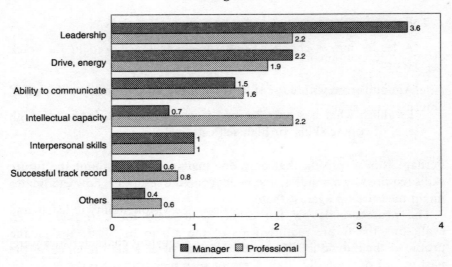

Figure 1.1 Selection criteria for general managers

How to choose potential general managers

Successful managers have a wide variety of approaches in identifying and choosing potential general managers. The most frequently mentioned (35 per cent) was examining the past record to find examples of a high success rate in a number of different roles. Comments like 'the ability to achieve exceptional goals and results', or 'evidence of team leading' were quite typical. In order of frequency of mention the following list shows the range of views:

1. Past record
2. No clear view – use of judgement
3. Provide early opportunities of experience
4. Interview
5. Profile, psychometric tests
6. Management development/succession plans
7. Observation against a profile
8. Personal knowledge

The diversity of replies is diminished by broadly grouping these under the headings listed above. However some of the quotes give a flavour:

'Recognise the potential and take a chance'

'A leader makes change. Look for changes achieved in the track record'

'Appoint from within, or at least from the same industry – it is safer'

'Establish what has been learned from experiences. Is there a high level of coping skills, or high self esteem?'

Perhaps it is surprising that only one manager talked about the future skills required by managers, and endeavoured to establish how candidates might measure up against these.

The professionals on the other hand were more thoughtful in evaluating the future requirements of the job to be filled, against the profile of the individual. However, they still place a high reliance on the past record of the individual. A senior search consultant said:

'when we begin a search for a senior general manager we would normally concentrate first on the business sector covered by the job highlighting those with a good track record that might be willing to move . . . A successful manager in a manufacturing company may well be quite inappropriate in the service sector.'

However this is just the beginning.

Again there was a wide variety of views about the best way to choose a general manager which I have grouped under headings and arranged in order of those mentioned most frequently by search consultants and advisors. These are:

1. Track record
2. Assessment Centres, multiple assessments
3. Profile against job requirements
4. Interview and judgement
5. Look for emotional resilience
6. Leadership record, relationships

Some of the comments made help us to understand better what the professionals are looking for:

'Look for excellence in what they are doing'

'Ability to cope under pressure'

'Leadership and success in at least two roles'

'360° assessment (i.e. of subordinate, peer and superior) against predetermined competencies'

'Multiple assessment programmes giving tests of ability and personality together with an appraisal of past work record'

'Ability to understand the minds of others'

'The ability to learn from mistakes'

Amongst the other responses one reply strongly emphasised the need for integrity in the individual as being very important.

It is not surprising that the two groups have a difference of emphasis as this will reflect the relative role in the selection process. There may well be a less-than-optimal solution where professionals are not used in the process at all. This is recognised by the managers who observed that their record of success in appointing successful general managers was pretty pedestrian with just over half claiming a good or high success rate.

Time allocation

There was a wide variety of time allocations amongst the managers reflecting to some degree the nature of their role and of the company. For example the leader of an advertising agency spends half his time with customers reinforcing service and the importance of relationships. Many managers will 'overclaim' the amount of time spent on strategic issues. The range of times spent strategically was from 10 per cent to 50 per cent with the average at 23 per cent which exactly matched the expectations of the professionals.

Perhaps the only real surprise was the low allocation of time devoted to management development and to personal development by managers. On average managers spend only 8 per cent of their time on management development and a further 4 per cent on personal development. Looking at the allocation of time to controlling, managers allocate 25 per cent on average to this function, but some overseas managers in India and Europe will spend more than half their time controlling. This is in contrast with the much smaller 18 per cent expected by the professionals. Full details of the comparison of time allocations are shown in Figure 1.2.

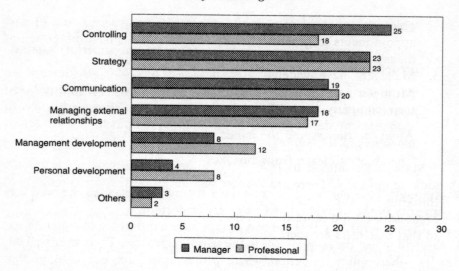

Figure 1.2 Comparison of time allocation

Summary of survey

There are some observations that flow from the survey which have implications for managers wishing to show continued improvement in performance. They are especially important as the source of greatest competitive advantage is found in the quality of the people resource. Increasingly this will be the performance differentiator in the future. The major observations are:

1. The methods of finding, preparing, and enabling new general managers are in many cases random and sub-optimal. Preparation for the important first general management role was not forthcoming for most newly appointed respondents.
2. There are important differences of view between the professional advisors and practising managers on the most important character-istics for successful general managers.
3. The requirements for general managers of the future are likely to be based on a different set of criteria for success than those used at present. This is not yet widely recognised in current practice.
4. There are wide differences in the methods adopted in choosing potential general managers. In only a very few cases have attempts been made to identify future requirements and match these against an

objective appraisal of a candidate's skills. The success rate of new appointments to general management roles, as judged by the senior managers in the survey, was about 50 per cent.

5. Managers have widely different allocations of time devoted to particular roles, which to some extent reflects their background, and their company needs. A very small amount of time is devoted to management development or personal development by the senior managers in this survey.

Managers continue to focus on the difficult tasks of today mainly looking inwardly. There are so many urgent, important tasks today that thinking of the future often takes a back seat. Given 'flatter' organisations and more direct reports, decisions are more complex too, so that managers are increasingly pressured to spend immediate time on 'pressing issues'. As an example, a UK manager from an industry that is restructuring observed, 'I have not had the luxury of time to spend on strategy or thinking too deeply about the future. If I don't get through the next two years, the future will be short and bleak!'

Lessons from successful companies

How do these results compare with observations of successful companies from around the world?

Lessons from the successful companies of our time show that the greatest winners are those that have found a way of destabilising the industry equilibrium by finding new ways to compete, or rewriting the rules of engagement in an industry. This gives the winning firm the ability to turn to advantage the way that they play the game. These winners have also held highly ambitious goals for their organisation far beyond those which seemed rationally achievable at the time these were conceived. They were able to 'think the unthinkable', then to set about achieving this.

Added to this, a number of highly successful companies have been able to spot new areas in which to compete that were a natural extension of the genuine competences that resided within their organisation. By spotting these opportunities early and applying the appropriate commitment and resource, they were able to achieve a winning position in fast-growing areas. These are truly growth companies that have outperformed those of their peer group which have, by necessity, spent their time on cost-cutting and restructuring. They are outward- rather than inward-looking, focusing on how they can deliver value to their customers, today, tomorrow and into the foreseeable future.

Something else is shared by these successful companies: the importance placed on finding and motivating the finest talent of people both at management level and at the 'coal face'. They place a high priority on lifting the skill base of the people and freeing them to make decisions as close as possible to the point of impact. As an example, Motorola has established what is, in effect, a corporate university to establish a high level of skills in their workforce.

Looking forward

We very much need to look forward to the environment of the future if we are to have a good feel for the skills that we expect our future general managers to have. There is a fair consensus, at least in general terms, of the worldwide environment which business people can expect. First, it will be a world of rapid change or of 'permanent white water' in which the unexpected will happen and circumstances will conspire to drive us off course. This does not negate the need to plan or to think about the future of course, rather the opposite. We need a clear sense of direction so that when the unexpected happens we make appropriate adjustments to regain the goals which we have set for ourselves.

Second, companies will need to be adept at operating with increased complexity. They will need to be comfortable with disparate and new technologies, seeing the advantages implicit for their company in being first in their arena to take advantage of them. It is not too dramatic to observe that there is before us an emerging environmental revolution that will profoundly change modern industry. The impact of information technology, of genetic engineering making available new materials, and also of intelligent machines, will all produce fundamentally new challenges and opportunities for today's business firms. Knowledge is a key concept that will be a telling factor. An important dimension of complexity is the increasing requirement to use judgement to optimise between apparently conflicting aims. Think about the opposing tensions of the following examples:

short run	vs	long run
development	vs	cost-cutting
shareholder value	vs	interests of wider stakeholders
company	vs	community
variety	vs	low cost
profit motive	vs	environment

Increasingly, managers of the future will need to be comfortable with conflicting aims and confident of their ability to optimise from these.

Third, the increasing trend towards internationalism will have an impact on companies that see themselves as being purely a national player. There will be lessons to be learnt from other countries, perhaps new entrants to compete with from outside, new alliances forged that will require a knowledge of the wider world and a strong empathy to other cultures.

Fourth, increasingly demanding customers will require a step change in response from manufacturers or suppliers. Consumers want more variety without cost penalty and they want the product they see *now*. They will not wait. They are better-informed, broadly through global communications for example, and will increasingly be capable of making accurate, direct comparisons of products through home-based electronic systems. Customers want faster and faster response, less product risk with time and cost taken out of the complete supply chain. Manufacturers, as well as service providers, will need to respond to this. Those that do so best will be the winners.

Fifth, it is certain that greater service will be an important differentiator, the source of most added value, or of competitive advantage. Companies will increasingly see that they sell a service of which the product forms a part – albeit an important one.

Sixth, companies will need to recognise that management and labour will not be available in the way they are today. There is, for example, a demographic time-bomb in the United Kingdom which means that there will be fewer people available to join the workforce and university graduates will be in relatively short supply. In the latter case, this will correspond with a sustained increase in demand due to the requirement of a more intellectually able management. Work patterns will also be different as employees at all levels will increasingly require a greater say in how they will work, where they work and the allocation of time between personal pursuits and company. On the shop floor, an annual hours contract will be normal; in the office, job-shares will not seem unusual. The firm needs both to understand the changes that are likely in the next five or ten years here and to think through the implications.

The picture painted here is not a universal prescription for all companies around the world. It is, however, a distillation of key trends that can be gleaned from the best work of those who have written on this topic and matches the author's experience in a worldwide theatre. Perhaps the most important contribution this section makes is the stimulation of readers to think through the key waves of influence that will impact on their individual business. This is just the first step because the thinking this provokes needs to be carried through to the implications or factors to take into account.

Implications for future managers

We need to understand first that if changes are needed in an organisation requiring managers to be re-skilled, this takes time. In a way, the future is with us now because we need to prepare now, even to be halfway ready for the changes that we can already see as inevitable. What, then, are the implications for our future managers?

The very first and perhaps most fundamental implication is that a winning company will need to build up its management base by maximising its intellectual energy and gaining the total commitment of its people. This does not mean that managers of the future will be rocket scientists or have MENSA IQs but it does mean that thinking is important. It will not be enough to build up a stock of management techniques or of being expert in deductive reasoning, as taught at business schools. Successful management in the future will encompass discontinuous or lateral thinking and creative solutions to break the mould. This will be coupled with the ability 'to do', actually to deliver and not just pontificate with theories of the future or abstracts devoid of reality. This is truly important.

Second, leadership is vital, specifically the ability to lead, motivate and excite a team of people to a common goal. Leadership is a key dimension of a successful manager today. Looking forward, this is a critical role which has a number of facets that will be increasingly important in the future. Selection of the appropriate goal of the firm, of the balanced team, of the core competences that will be essential for the delivery of a superior growth-led strategy. All this will be essential, as will a high degree of personal commitment and of motivational qualities to lead the team to higher levels of performance than ever they dreamed. At the end of this, the truly successful leader will hear his team members say 'see what we have achieved'. Leadership can be silent.

Third is strategic capability. Firms that rely on entrenched positions or a monopoly of resources will not fare well in the future. The winners will be those that can think and act strategically. Key to this is the development of core competences that can be used for future growth. This bundle of skills and knowledge will enable the firm to establish long-lasting, winning ways with customers.

Fourth is the ability to communicate. The old adage 'you must be good and be seen to be good' is true in business. If a leader is to rally troops about him at a time when change is all around and when the international dimension increasingly matters then ability to communicate takes prime time even from a busy leader. This is time-consuming stuff. It is hard work. It is essential. Coupled with this priority of communication is an empathy for cultural diversity. Everyone knows the horror stories of miscommunication which haunt the international débutante manager. However, any message delivered personally or through available media, no matter how correct, will lose impact without the warmth of affinity with other cultures.

The fifth area of focus for future managers I have called curiosity. Managers of the future will not confine their thinking to prescribed boxes but will wish to see early new trends, new opportunities which evolve from an insatiable curiosity with all that surrounds them. Naturally they must refine the raw trends for implications but they must be curious about disparate disciplines, varied vectors of influence, of worldwide windows. They will not begrudge the time to travel and experience, they will not see as a chore the need to read widely, they will never presume to be knowledgeable enough to stop learning.

For me, these are the five most important areas of competence for our general managers of the future. They are not necessarily those which are held in highest regard today. Neither do they accord with the views expressed by managers in the survey. Further, too few top managers are devoting sufficient time to these critical areas. I predict that the winners of the next decade will have thought more carefully and comprehensively about the skill sets they need to succeed in the future.

Future music

Many of the themes that have been touched on in this chapter are picked up and developed later in this book. There are no watertight compartments in general management and readers will see some of the themes developed in much more detail elsewhere. When we are looking to the future and reflecting on the requirements for managers, Management and Leadership (Chapter 2), The Environment (Chapter 5) and Taking Charge (Chapter 9), are very pertinent, developing more fully themes introduced here. However this represents future music which will be played out later in the book.

2 Management or Leadership?

Management or leadership?

What tasks or attributes do we categorise under each of these headings? If we can segregate duties under these two headings will it help managers to be more successful? In fact, de-aggregation is not very helpful in giving a manager pointers for success, just as dictionary definitions are unhelpful. One way that helps managers to gain a real understanding of the scope of leadership in contrast to management, is to build word pictures that stimulate our thinking. A good example of word pictures is shown in Figure 2.1 which is used by a specialist consulting firm, People Change Organisation (PCO).

Management tasks

Management and leadership are not mutually exclusive and the general manager, in whatever setting, will have both qualities. There are specific tasks of management that have been clear throughout time and will be well-mastered by the able general manager. These are largely fact-related. As a reminder, it is convenient to combine these areas of management into five main headings.

1. *Planning*. In all that we do , the forward thinking about the issues, the alternatives and the desired end result will help us to set appropriate goals against which later progress can be measured. Management literature has listed a variety of specific techniques to help this process.
2. *Budgeting*, which of course is part of the process of planning but is worthy of separate identification. In most firms the detailed budgeting process will be annual and financial and will be a key process for the organisation. This is, of course, linked to the process of strategy.

Management	*versus*	*Leadership*
Not emotional		Passionate visionary
Tell		Ask
Talk		Listen
Expect less		Encourage more
Trust difficult		Trust easy
Calming		Enthusiasm
Know the answers		Open to suggestions
Tells how		Shares why
Directs		Points the way
Has subordinates		Has followers
Sees detail		Sees overall view
Systems centred		People centred
How and why		What and why
Maintains		Originates
Controls		Inspires
Stands apart		Seeks company
Goals/plans		Identity/values
Doing the job right		Doing the right job
Good soldier		Own person
Eyes on bottom line		Eyes on horizon
Aims for security		Enjoys change
Structured		Flexible
Accepts the status quo		Challenges the status quo

Without managers the vision of leaders remain dreams. Leaders need managers to convert visions into realities. For continuous success organisations need both managers and leaders, however, as most seem to be over-managed and under-led, they need to find ways of having both at the same time. Perhaps the best way to handle this paradox is for managers to aim to be managers when viewed from above and leaders when viewed from below, and to remember that the need for leadership grows as we move up the organisation. This is only one of the challenges that can make working life fun.

(Reproduced with permission of PCO.)

Figure 2.1   Management/leadership comparison

3. *Organising* by putting in place a formal structure to achieve the end results envisaged in the planning phase. Separate objectives from the budget will be set for individuals within the organisation.
4. The creation of *incentive programmes*. In my view, this is an essential area which requires careful consideration in getting the blend of benefits which support the key thrusts of the business. Communication of the benefits of the incentive programme must be clear and must be seen to support the main thrusts of the business plan. Clearly, incentives must be compatible with the goals and so constructed as to act as an incentive.
5. *Controlling*. This is often the area that comes first to the mind of the newly appointed general manager as he worries about how to control his new domain. This process involves the continuous measurement of variations from key agreed measures that were specified in the planning phase. Exception reporting and detailed monthly accounts will give the information to review results within the time horizon that is appropriate for the particular area under the spotlight.

Leadership

Being appointed a manager makes one a boss but it does not make anyone a leader. It is clear today that good management on its own is not sufficient for a manager to succeed in this fast-changing world. Much more is required which we can broadly ascribe to aspects of leadership. We look for vision, strategy, enthusiasm, ability to motivate others, a thirst for knowledge and continuous improvement and the setting of demanding goals. Leadership is increasingly recognised as the factor most crucial to success in general management yet it is pretty difficult to define in an operational sense. If it is difficult to define, it is more difficult to isolate the factors that would early identify potential leaders. Those who use psychological testing as an indicator, will recognise the difficulty of setting objective tests when the definition of the end-product is so fuzzy.

However, there is universal support for the view that leadership qualities are perhaps the most significant factors influencing a general manager's success. This was illustrated in the international review of general managers described in Chapter 1 where leadership skills rated the highest priority. This is increasingly true given the stresses of change in a fast-moving world when it is not enough to simply have a store-chest of specific skills to deal with each new challenge as it occurs. Leadership provides a capability throughout an organisation that welds together a team that can respond to changes positively or indeed induce change for the firm's benefit. While some people try to define concisely the concept of leadership, most would argue that there is more value in looking at different aspects of leadership to provide inspiration or food for thought for those who don the leadership mantle.

Perhaps, given the importance of this topic and the direct relevance to managers today, it would be reasonable to expect business schools to devote a high proportion of the course to the subject. This is usually not true as most of the MBA programmes remain heavily biased to sequential thinking and the building of an armoury of technical skills. Part of the reason for this is that the teaching of leadership is reliant on learning experiences, on awareness and creative thinking. These are less easy to teach effectively and case studies are seldom deep enough to provide a real experience.

If we are to define leadership it will only be of very limited value, pointing to some characteristics. A definition like that in Collins' Dictionary tells us that 'leadership is the art of being a leader'. A leader is 'a person that leads, guides or inspires others'. This definition does not really help us to understand the dimensions that will help us to perform better. There are attributes of leadership that will be recognisable but there is also an unseen dimension that is difficult to describe. It is a bit like describing an excellent painting. The physical aspects of the painting can be easily described, but the spirit of the painting that transforms it from the ordinary to the excellent is much more difficult.

Attributes of leadership

To provide greater awareness of practical measures that help understand leadership more deeply, I have grouped the dimensions into five main headings. These are shown in a simplified form in Figure 2.2. I have called these: defining a vision, commitment to success, communication, challenging the status quo and personal characteristics. I will deal with each of these in turn.

First, *defining a vision* is the initial stage which is absolutely essential if the team are to perform to the common goal. While the input will arise from members of the team, from outside analytical help and from a careful scanning of trends, the commitment and ownership of the vision must be the leader's. The best leaders are capable of thinking the unthinkable and of picking up innovation even though the initial ideas may not have originated with them. They will have a high curiosity level

Successful Management

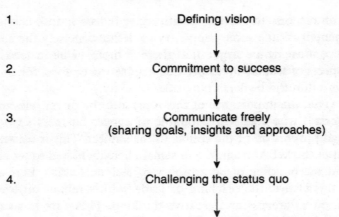

1.   Defining vision

2.   Commitment to success

3.   Communicate freely
(sharing goals, insights and approaches)

4.   Challenging the status quo

5.   Develop personal characteristics of leadership
(learn the skills)

Figure 2.2   Five dimensions of leadership

and will be well-informed from their own network of contacts and wide reading. They are not afraid of change, but rather view this as an environmental factor that can give the initiative to their own organisation.

Once the vision has been defined the means to its realisation must be provided. These include the right team with the appropriate variety of skills, and an organisation in which they can put these skills to use. The people must be empowered through ensuring that they have the appropriate skill base and also by ensuring that the organisation structure is appropriate.

The second attribute of leadership is a *commitment to success*. The leader typically has high energy and drive, a fact which was also picked up in the international survey that is used as resource for this book. The commitment to success is not just about enthusiasm, drive and the will to win, it is also about the hard work of preparation. I can still remember today the words of my rugby coach in New Zealand who reminded the team 'the will to win is important but the will to prepare is vital'.

Third, is the need to *communicate openly* and freely. There is a requirement to share information on the goals, any adjustment to the pathway towards the goals or any new initiatives that are compatible with them. Too often, the leader may well have changed direction without proper communication to find his troops marching forward to the precipice that he would like to avoid. The communication is of course two-way and will be styled to have appropriate impact. It is especially good for stories of success to be shared so that wins in some areas can be shared with others. Equally, where there are failures, these should become 'learning experiences' from which the team can benefit.

Fourth, is *challenging the status quo*. This is worthy of separation from other attributes because it strikes at the root of many areas where leadership is required. The 'not invented here' syndrome is alive and well in many organisations today. Young managers are still put off by the old managerial hands who remind these bright, young, naive souls that 'we don't do things like that around here'. Whether it be finding creative solutions in the market, challenging strategy or invoking business process re-engineering, there remains a need to challenge the status quo.

Finally, as a catch-all, I have grouped together a number of *personal characteristics* that are found in successful leaders. As the basis for highlighting here, I have included those identified in the literature on leadership, from personal observation and those discerned by the search consultants who recruit senior general managers. The personal characteristics most frequently highlighted in successful leaders are:

- flexibility;
- ability to inspire others;
- enthusiasm;
- ability to build relationships;
- ability to inspire trust;
- ability to communicate;
- ability to delegate;
- willingness to experiment;
- frankness;
- integrity.

Missing from this generic list is intellect, not because it is unimportant, but rather because the role of leader is wide and it is not always essential to have high intellect. However, in business it is clear that the effective leader needs to have both the intellect and the conceptual capacity to deal with the scope of his job.

Leader, born or bred?

You have heard the expression many times, 'he was a born leader'. Is it the case that leaders are born and not bred? The evidence would suggest that the attributes of leadership can be acquired through study and lifetime experiences. This is not to deny the influencing process of early years which can significantly shape the character of the person. In my own case, being second eldest in a family of four boys certainly shaped determination, a competitive spirit and a need to be noticed! However, much more important for leadership in the business world are the experiences accumulated over time. The richer and wider the early experiences, the better prepared will be the candidate for general management.

The research from different countries gave an unexpected insight, namely, that managers who gained their initial experiences in a 'small pool' often received a breadth of knowledge not always available in a larger pool. Internationally experienced managers from Australia, Israel and New Zealand spoke of their ability to see the complete business chain very early on. In contrast with their peers in Europe and USA, they received a more general introduction compared with the refinement of deep knowledge over a smaller part of the business system, whilst the Europeans and Americans were often better prepared by technique in a specialty area but had to wait until much later to gain the wider experience. In fact, nationality strongly influences the development of different characteristics. In Australia, Israel, South Africa and New Zealand for example there is a very strong competitive spirit. This desire to win, almost despite the odds, will overlay other country characteristics which can be recognised in individuals. This 'will to win' is equally present in many of those who have been serious team players in a sporting environment.

The concept of strong leaders coming from a smaller environment is not altogether a novel one. In the early 1990s Victor and Mildred Goertzel, in their work *Cradles of Eminence*, reviewed several hundred successful people to see what they had in common. In almost every case they came from small towns and were driven by ambition.

New cultures also provide a rich source of learning as managers need to deal with a different theatre of operation. They will learn to challenge yet be empathetic to different cultures if they are to be successful in working through other people. It is for this reason that geographic moves for a high-flying potential general manager are very valuable. This experience will help to provide flexibility to deal with people in a different way yet to achieve goals within the same tight time-scale.

Lessons for new managers

The starting-point must be to examine yourself. The old adage goes 'So you want to manage – first try managing yourself.' People want to be led, not managed. They prefer encouragement and challenge to close control or continuous measurement. There is a preference for the carrot rather than the stick. If the managers are to manage themselves they must first understand their strengths and their weaknesses. This means knowing yourself objectively and well so that your mental image of yourself matches that held by your peer group or your boss. Clearly, leading from one's strengths is key and understanding how to ameliorate weaknesses is also important. This latter area may be best overcome by a combination of self-preparation, coaching and ensuring that one's supporting team has complementary strengths. A self-development programme is of great importance and while the company must sign off to lend its full support, I believe that the responsibility for initiating self-development rests with the individual. The young manager's career development and therefore self-development plans are far too important to be left to the company, no matter how strong the career development focus of the personnel department or of the Chief Executive.

Prior to the first general management appointment, the young executive will have endeavoured to get a wide variety of experiences. In gaining this experience, balance must be struck between getting sufficient variety and staying in a post sufficiently long to gain a reasonable depth of experience. Broadening experiences are the best pathway to prepare for the leadership role.

The role of mentors to new managers has been well-publicised, for, like non-executive directors, they act as father-figures. While I like the concept, in my experience and that of many managers to whom I have spoken, this may be over-rated as a useful formula for success, and is sometimes used as a crutch to offset a lack of proper preparation. Mentors may well provide encouragement and a sense of balance when the new manager is immersed in so many areas requiring attention. However, the ability of the mentor to provide either the input or the time to understand the issues is often missing. Equally, if the mentor is the role model as well, this may well limit the capacity of the new manager.

As an example, a manager in a New Zealand subsidiary company had been identified to succeed the managing director some four years earlier than the retirement date of the incumbent. The candidate about to be appointed to his first general-manager role recognised the insularity of his experience which was limited to New Zealand, and also the limitation of having only the one role model. This was remedied by arranging a three-year term in an overseas company, while still maintaining a mentor link with the New Zealand-based managing director.

On balance, the concept of a mentor is a good one and has benefited many well-known, high-profile managers of our day. However, it requires from both parties an investment of time which is seldom given in practice. The role of mentor is best seen therefore as providing balance or encouragement rather than coaching in technique.

Experience

A good manager learns a great deal from different experiences or learning situations. These learning experiences are valuable even where mistakes are made. In times of adversity or where things go wrong there are valuable opportunities to learn. Picking up the major lessons from these events is positive and must be distinguished from agonising after a decision with the thought 'if only I had done this differently'. Equally, developing managers will learn a lot from their boss. They will watch the decisions made, watch the boss at work and secretly try their own decision-making capability in the privacy of their own mind. Perhaps the best boss from whom to learn is one that is truly capable in many different areas but who has some glaring weaknesses too. Certainly, one of the skills that all managers must learn is how to handle their boss. This will require knowledge of both parties' preferred style of working to see the different strengths and weaknesses of each participant.

Lessons

There are some lessons from successful managers about their approach to work. These include:

1. Prepare well. Do not begin without knowing where you wish to finish. Think thoroughly first and then act. However, be aware of the disease of 'analysis paralysis' and make sure that the thinking is commensurate with the importance of the decision.
2. Make sure that you have, or that you acquire, the tools to make you successful. These will include your knowledge of the industry and the key players in it. It will include a knowledge of your firm, its strategy and your objectives. Also, it will include the relationships within the firm so that you are aware of the pivotal points to get things done.
3. Identify the key personal skills needed in the job and ensure that you are well-equipped in the critical areas.

4. Have high personal standards and a high integrity because your reputation is your most valuable asset. Be prepared to work hard and be seen as an achiever.
5. Ensure that you have a continuous personal development plan that has the support of the firm.
6. Make sure that you build into your programme time for reflection and wider thinking.

Inspirational and perspirational leadership

Initially, I preferred to think within the context of managing a multinational organisation in terms of charismatic leadership and technocratic leadership. The former is the visionary, motivational aspect while technocratic leadership is about the basis for achievement. However this is capable of misunderstanding as the charismatic aspects are sometimes seen as synonymous with heroic leadership which applies only to high-profile outstanding people. This is of course too limiting and work has been published on the 'post-heroic leadership' that emphasises the empowerment of a team of people rather than focusing on one individual. The use of a team of motivated individuals is an exceptionally valuable and effective way of achieving corporate aims. For the purpose of this section I have elected to break down leadership into *in*spirational and *per*spirational.

In multinational businesses especially there is a need for a breed of leadership that regrettably remains in short supply. It needs to be 'inspirational' (charismatic), imparting a vision and defining strategies to achieve this. The 'perspirational' (technocratic) provides the practical basis for achievement. Both are needed. Some features of an *inspirational leader* are as follows:

1. The leader practises management by walking around because leaders need to be visible and use opportunities through questions and statements to reinforce the culture and objectives.
2. The leader is a role model for other leaders and is transparent in decision-making and uses symbolic behaviour.
3. The leader is a living ethical standard, aware that his/her actions are always under public scrutiny.
4. The leader is an *agent provocateur*, a non-conformist and an agent for change.

5. Every leader needs apostles who are equally energised and committed to the same cause. The leader needs feedback.
6. The leader recognises the importance of excellent communication inside as well as outside the organisation. This requires a heavy allocation of time.
7. The leader is able to fight bureaucracy without destroying essential control.

The *perspirational leadership* aspect is equally important if we want action. If there is only the inspirational, the whole organisation will be psyched up but will go nowhere because there is no enablement. Standards of achievement are the currency of the vision. Tools are needed to achieve this. For example, we need:

1. Organisational clarity and clarity of objectives.
2. Reward systems to be aligned with the goals.
3. Compatibility of resource allocation and deployment. Procedures need to be right and knowledge transferred through networking. People need to be placed first with a meritocracy that ensures that the best get ahead.
4. Controls and the ability to measure to ensure that the business is being measured on the correct basis. Individuals and teams must always be able to track their own performance.

In summary, successful international leaders do not just lead, neither do they just manage. Both tasks must be undertaken. The vision must be connected to the mundane tools. In this setting, the leader achieves this through team-building, through openness and feedback. Every media device that is relevant will be used to promulgate the message from personal visits to videos, team briefings, magazines and special events. Top appointments will remain the prerogative of the leader and must be seen to reflect the underlying corporate message. Initiatives compatible with the strategy will be chosen and must be seen to be supported. For example, if customer service is high on the corporate agenda, the leader must be visible in visits to customers. The leader will cause discomfort by creating comparisons with outside companies through the process of 'bench-marking'. The company will be led to strive to be best in its field, challenging performance as well as elements of strategy. There is no comfort zone by living with the status quo, for this will lead to the eventual decline of the company. These are all tasks of leaders, especially those who work in international settings.

Leadership – the unseen factor

Most business people would claim to recognise effective leadership in practice, and so they should, when they rate this aspect so highly in selecting future managers. Yet, as we have seen, the definition of leadership is not easy, which is why we have tried to look at the essence of it in this chapter. In an endeavour to capture the nub of leadership other cultures deal with this in a different way. W. Chan Kim and Renee A. Mauborgne captured some very interesting new insights in their July–August 1992 *Harvard Business Review* article on 'Parables of Leadership'. Their parables try to illustrate the essential qualities of leadership and the acts that portray a leader.

They talk, for example, about the ability to hear what is left unspoken and of the importance of humility and commitment. Examples are given which show the value of looking at reality from differing vantage points. In another illustration, the authors demonstrate how true leadership sustains as it goes quietly about its task, producing a superior long-term result compared with the intense but spasmodic displays of leadership than can sometimes be seen.

Of course, the concept of the leader being 'unseen' is neither novel nor new, for many management writers have observed that leadership is at its best when it appears to be unseen – almost non-existent. Leaders are at their best when they draw from those around them excellence and commitment that the team may not have been fully aware of. I like the way that Albert Schweitzer, the philosopher, puts it. He observes 'The true worth of man is not to be found in man himself but in the colours and texture that come alive in others.' This, in my experience, is a key factor found in successful leaders whether they be in a commercial, political or recreational setting.

The constituent's view

Effective leadership involves the whole organisation which must be motivated to perform. It is therefore helpful to dwell for a moment on the reaction of those different constituents receiving the message. It is important to recognise that followers have a choice, about how committed they will be to the leader's doctrine. In reality, people *choose* to lead and people will *choose* to follow so that regard must be paid to the aspirations and hopes of the humans at each end of the process. The leader needs to be credible which means he must really understand the needs of those who are helping to transform the enterprise to achieve its new goals. Hand-in-glove with credibility goes integrity. A considerable amount of time will therefore be needed in communication at all levels. There is an unavoidably high labour content for leaders, especially where significant change is involved.

It will readily be seen that those who choose to follow will do so more perfectly if they have loyalty – first, to the company, then to the leader. Loyalty is not something that a boss can command, he must earn it and retain it by continually building on the bond of trust between them. Kouges and Posner conducted research amongst 15 000 people around the world focusing on those on the receiving end of leadership initiatives. They found that the ten most used words of how people felt when working with leaders were:

1. valued
2. motivated
3. enthusiastic
4. challenged
5. inspired
6. capable
7. supported
8. powerful
9. respected
10. proud.

To maintain the high motivation, the thinking leader is constantly helping constituents to top up their skill base with new opportunities for education, new experiences and information. They need to feel involved, believe in the goals and their ability to achieve them. The more confident the organisation becomes, the higher their ability to deliver. Leaders must stay in touch and be understanding of the needs of those that follow them.

Trust

Warren Bennis in his book, *On Becoming a Leader* (1990), reflects on the importance of integrity as a key ingredient in the make up of a leader. He observes that leaders have four characteristics which generate and sustain trust:

1. *Constancy* There should be no surprises for the group. The messages should be consistent.
2. *Congruity* A leader will have no gaps between what he says and what he does. His actions will support his words.
3. *Reliability* Leaders are not fair-weather friends but they are around when the going is tough, when support is needed, and it really counts.
4. *Integrity* There is an imperative for leaders to honour their commitments and their promises.

These are four important factors, but in my view the greatest of all of them is integrity. This is the very core of trust and it must be reflected in actions of the leader, and incorporated into the total culture. Trust is hard to earn, hard to maintain yet easy to lose by falling down on any of the factors that support it.

The management of change

Change – inevitable and accelerating

There are good reasons to think about the management of change separately. First, because change is inevitable, is all around and is accelerating. Second, because there are some special areas of focus which will help the general manager be much more effective in this environment. Third, traditional management skills are usually inadequate to deal with both the speed and the process of change.

Most people dislike change. It interrupts a smooth pattern of equilibrium, and it creates stresses and uncertainties that many would prefer to avoid. Is it possible that we have seen the greatest intensity of change and that the pressures will diminish in future years? I think not. First, the concept of living with change is not a new one. Heraclitus, in 500 BC, observed that 'all is flux' and that 'the only constant is change'. Today, there is much evidence both in literature and from observation that supports the view that change is taking place at a faster pace than ever and that this is likely to continue into the next millennium. Factors most often mentioned in support of this view include:

- a more global economy with faster transference of ideas, products and technologies;
- the exponential growth of the information age and the capability to take advantage of change rapidly;
- the growing trend to openness and deregulation;

- the market demand for more individual products or services shortening product life-cycles and manufacturing runs with a consequent prize for innovation and speed of response.

Implications

Dealing with the more direct implications for executives, I would make three observations. First, the management of change must be an integral part of the skill base of the modern executive. The question becomes 'how can we take advantage of change?' rather than 'do we have to be concerned about it as a special topic?' It is therefore helpful to look at the management skill base and the organisation to see that these are compatible with change. Second, we need to look at some key business processes to see if these need to be re-engineered given the new setting. Third, it is helpful to gain insights into the management of change in practice in situations which all executives will recognise. The management of change certainly demands the very finest leadership skills that can be delivered by an executive. It also requires a disciplined, methodical approach if the leader is to focus on the key tasks and retain strong emotional resilience.

Taking advantage of change

The innovators of old did not wait for change to occur and then think about the implications of this. They recognised that if they created purposeful change they could often outplay the competition by altering the rules of the game. Indeed, this approach is one of the factors that causes change.

We will see in Chapter 6 (see Figure 6.2) that within the dimensions of management there are many core competences that successful managers need to demonstrate and which are the foundation for success in a rapidly changing world. At this time we wish to dwell on any special skill areas that are helpful as managers initiate, facilitate and manager the change process.

Teams

Teams and major change are an inevitable combination. The double benefit for managers who are involved in teams which focus on a particular problem or opportunity is, first, the fact that well-balanced teams outperform individuals. Second, they also gain from the development experience of working in an exciting, special environment. Great value is obtained from teams working across individual business boundaries in a group perhaps dealing with special geographic growth areas like China, India, Russia or Indonesia, or special projects covering a number of business units. A good example of the use of teams is shown in the case study 'On Taking Charge at Coats Viyella' included in Chapter 9.

Not only do teams achieve great results on the chosen projects but they also strengthen the performance of the members, broaden their horizons and improve management processes. The unique social dimension is supportive and adds to corporate bonding and networking within a diverse corporation.

Factors for the future

We have already recognised the fast-moving world with greater competition, more use of information technology and a greater worldwide involvement by most companies. In this role, successful managers and leaders will have:

- The technical ability to carry out the defined tasks.
- Conceptual ability to deal in the abstract and to think afresh thus arriving at an imaginative vision and plan of action.
- A sufficiently wide breadth of contact and ability to tap the environment to be continually aware of factors which will cause timely change and sources of value creation. It is important to be international in outlook.
- Interpersonal skills and the ability to communicate will need to be well-honed so that the team are motivated and highly charged to achieve the common goal.
- A desire to experiment, to test new situations, acting quickly and decisively. Learning experiences from 'failures' will be valued provided that they were not due to sloppy, inappropriate, thoughtless actions.

Dealing especially with the environment of rapid change, the managers of the future will have to be very adept at handling more than one variable at a time. They will need to manage the existing business to short-term aims and targets yet putting effort behind major change through strategy shifts or business process re-engineering. This is a major challenge across a multi-product, multi-geographic company as the followers need to hear a simple message clearly communicated. Managers are not well-prepared to make optimal decisions from goals that are often in conflict.

It is also clear that technology is impacting more rapidly on business opportunities and the way we conduct business. The leadership challenge is to use this proactively and competently, rapidly developing new competences that will deliver competitive advantage. In general, new competences for the future will certainly be needed and these need to be thought about and pursued today. All this will need to be performed in a different work environment – shared databases, less support staff, using flatter organisations and with more work being carried out by many people at home. Organisations will change certainly away from functional to more holistic businesses with increasing challenge to current processes that do not add to the customer's perception of values. During these movements, expectations of stake-holders will also change to be more demanding, more apprehensive of new roles and with a greater need for leadership and direction. These are important elements which leaders will need to consider for the future.

There is no acceptable evidence that suggests that different educational backgrounds provide a better start for managers who are leaders. A good, high-quality background is preferred as a starting-point and if this is topped up with an MBA degree from a credible university this is very beneficial. However, as we have seen from the area traversed here, the best training is a wide variety of experiences, achieved as early as possible, preferably over different businesses and differing geography. Leaders continue to learn, develop and grow. They are at their best when the team is strong, confident and pointed in the same direction.

3   Management Development

Talent is the differentiator

What would you rather have? A business with unique physical resources such as access to special materials or processes protected through patents but with a stock of average managers or, on the other hand, a business with little to differentiate its physical base but with committed, outstanding people? The question is rhetorical because most people recognise that competitive advantage derived from physical assets is seldom maintained in the long run. On the other hand, *people* really do make a difference to delivery in the longer term.

We are all aware that the organisation that finds, develops and motivates talented people to a common goal will be a winner in the competitive world in which we operate. Why is it that some industries or, more particularly, some companies are able to find the key to building and retaining a stock of talented people? Is the answer to do with conditions of work which mitigate against some less technologically advanced industries or is it to do with pay and conditions? The answer of course is none of these. It is the excitement of the work place, the involvement in the future, the feeling of belonging that creates differentiation. The atmosphere is one of dissatisfaction with the status quo, providing a state of continuous learning or, as some writers put it, a 'learning organisation'.

Within this concept, learning is not about cramming the mind with even more facts but it is more to do with study, practice, feedback and change. There are some important and interesting projects being undertaken at the Massachusetts Institute of Technology (MIT) in Cambridge, Massachussets, which are currently being expanded with its new research work called 'inventing the organisations of the twenty-first century'. This forthcoming study is based on the contention that there will be dramatic changes in the way successful businesses are organised in the next century. Some companies will be well-positioned to exploit this while others will not. MIT hope to invent the new organisation that will be common in 10–20 years from now. The sort of projects they envisage include the following:

31

1. Inventing new organisational processes, especially those that take advantage of information technology.
2. The impact of ubiquitous information on the management of a company.
3. The role of organisational culture in organisational learning.
4. Managing the boundaryless corporation.

However, referring to the work that MIT has already done, there are some important lessons. First, they note that learning disciplines have a significant, measurable impact on a corporation's success. While there are many successes within the learning organisations, there are quite a number of disappointments. Disappointments are acceptable provided that they are treated as 'learning experiences'. They also observe that developing learning capabilities requires a blend of both behavioural and technical changes in the organisation. New conceptual skills are important and are developed in this atmosphere. Finally, they have a clear view that leadership arises from a deeply held personal conviction of those leading and those following.

People, above all else

I believe that there is a strong case to be made for all managers to devote a significant amount of time to finding, developing and motivating subordinates. This really is a genuine source of competitive advantage. It is an area where the manager can add true value, even though the pay-off might be in the frame of the medium or longer term which will prove a challenge to those with a very short term vision. Throughout much of the book the concept of motivating and empowering people has high attention. As we move to the future, the demands on management will be greater and the gap through differentiation of the best performing companies from the bunch will be larger. Companies today need to position themselves to be amongst the winners.

Continuous learning

How can a business leader create a setting that has the best chance of enhancing value for the company through developing superior people? The best start is for the leader to create the environment for continuous learning in their organisation. This, of course, starts with the leader who will already have recognised that the future holds a good deal of radical change in the way that work is done. He or she will realise that a cultural shift will be required because the skills for the future will be different, as will the demands on the people in the organisation.

Have leaders thought about the impact of the demands on managers, say in the next decade? They will see:

- faster change;
- more competition;
- greater customer demands;
- complex circumstances, often with choices that call for optimal solutions rather than black or white decision-making;
- new technology, processes;
- greater internationalism;
- more complex trading arrangements, partnerships and alliances;
- greater regulation and more deregulation in differing areas;
- more access to data and information.

Quite a formidable list that may daunt some people, yet for the experienced manager this is the environment that this natural or normal. The leaders of the next generation, according to Warren Bennis, will need to have the following attributes:

- a broad education;
- incalculable curiosity;
- boundless enthusiasm;
- belief in people and teamwork;
- willingness to take risks;
- devotion to long-term rather than short-term profit growth;
- commitment to excellence;
- readiness;
- virtue;
- vision.

They must be able to express themselves and be capable of making new moves in an international theatre. This list, in my view, is fairly complete but I believe that I would want to add two more. First, there needs to be a real sense of purpose to deliver the vision and all important elements of it. Second must be a great thirst for knowledge – beyond curiosity – for they must 'continuously journey yet never arrive'. The fun is in the travelling!

Continuous learning in an organisation is more complex than pulling a lever or commanding that this should happen. The organisation is driven from the top, embraced by the team who learn from the feedback of experiences. There is a feeling of openness of sharing, of excitement in organisations that have embraced the key elements which, for me, are:

- establishing a clear vision;
- empowering individuals to perform;
- learning from looking outward to trends and inward to self-improvement of the organisation;
- providing opportunities for team learning;
- ensuring a high level of communication through networking as well as the regular traditional channels.

Learning organisation

In *The Fifth Discipline* Peter Senge describes the five parts of a learning organisation broadly. Each plays an essential part in developing the right atmosphere for the learning and growth to take place:

1. *Systems thinking.* This is about inter-related actions or invisible fabrics which provide a conceptual framework or a body of knowledge that makes the pattern clearer.
2. *Personal mastery.* Senge recognises that mastery means achieving a special level of proficiency. Here there is a continuous clarification of one's personal vision and a deepening of the understanding of it. It becomes the focus for energies and the basis of priorities. The individuals need to develop patience and to develop their ability to see reality more clearly. There is usually a gap between the reality of today and the forward vision which needs to be closed by actions to achieve the goal, not by reducing expectations. This can be seen in Figure 3.1.

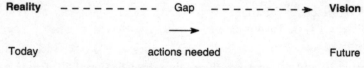

Figure 3.1   Reality gap

3. *Mental models.* These are the assumptions, generalisations, patterns or images that influence how we understand the world and which are the precursor to actions.
4. *Building shared visions.* It is a clearly recognised fact derived from empirical evidence all around us that leadership has inspired organisations over the years by holding a shared picture of the future which we wish to create.
5. *Team learning.* In an organisation the power of the team to enhance learning is great. The teams may be at their best when they are

purpose-built for a set objective and a set tenure. They will help to bring about the fundamental shift of <u>mindset that</u> is needed to break with the past and provide a giant step forward.

There is a powerful case for organisations to develop a spirit of continuous learning. It provides motivation, development opportunities for people and the environment where change can more readily be effected. Clearly, companies committed to learning will find it easier to recruit and <u>retain</u> the best talent. This will enhance performance immeasurably.

Managerial competences

Each management role in a company will emphasise different competences ahead of others depending upon the key contribution expected from the manager in the role. These go beyond the technical requirements that will be obvious from the nature of the position. A production manager of a new sophisticated plant in a brewery will need to understand the production process and have sufficient engineering understanding to be effective in the case of breakdowns or in planning maintenance to prevent such breakdown. This manager is likely to understand production scheduling, plant layout and new techniques. In addition to these tools of trade, there will be managerial competences, some of which are valued more highly than others in this role. To give a flavour of these in Figure 3.2, I have listed a fairly general inventory of managerial competences which are currently in use in Coats Viyella Plc. These headings are the basis of discussion at annual appraisal time when the key competences for the present role are discussed at the same time as the individual's performance is frankly discussed against previously agreed objectives.

The same list is also useful for managers who systematically wish to review general competences against their perception of strengths and weaknesses. It will, of course, require very objective self-insight or perhaps the input of a trusted mentor. If you are of a robust nature, ask your superiors, peers and subordinates to grade you on each heading.

Personnel input

The personnel function has been with us since at least the industrial revolution. Today, the role of this function varies according to the value placed on it by the company and, to a less extent, the capability of the

Figure 3.2

Leadership
- Has the ability to motivate individuals and teams to reach business objectives
- Delegates tasks appropriately and effectively
- Inspires a 'shared vision' or common set of goals
- Provides stability and direction
- Leaves specifics to others
- Constructively challenges the status quo

Results orientation
- Focuses attention on key objectives
- Sets specific goals for self and others
- Establishes a clear focus and direction
- Is able to act and make decisions in situations marked by risk and uncertainty
- Shows a bias for action
- Determines whether results have been achieved

Business strategy/development
- Takes a longer-term strategic view of business development
- Is aware of internal and external customer needs
- Has the ability to change in reaction to altered circumstances
- Recognises opportunities for action
- Identifies and assesses alternative courses of action

Change orientation
- Continuously monitors and evaluates activity
- Adjusts behaviour to suit new procedures and systems
- Obstacles to change are evaluated and measures to alleviate problems implemented
- Has the ability to modify opinions in the light of conflicting evidence
- Relevant people are encouraged to understand and participate in any changes made

People development
- Identifies the development needs of team members
- Designs or locates appropriate training programmes for people
- Gives people assignments or projects to develop their abilities
- Gives clear feedback
- Gives people latitude to do more challenging tasks to help them develop
- Monitors progress and provides support

Relationships/communications
- Considers impact of actions on team members
- Sensitive to needs and motives of other people
- Consistently ensures all necessary communication of plans and developments
- Exhibits confidence when handling people face to face
- Relates effectively to peers – and superiors
- Seeks to involve others in discussion and decision-making
- Communicates effectively both verbally and in writing

Judgement
- Makes sound and objective decisions
- Thinks through implications
- Identifies the key factor(s) in a complex problem
- Accepts responsibility for decision-making
- Takes decisions promptly or puts them off?

Knowledge
- Uses knowledge or experience in a way which helps maximise opportunities for the company
- Demonstrates a growing awareness and understanding of events and developments both inside and outside the company
- Takes active steps to increase professional and job-related knowledge

Source: Coats Viyella Plc

Figure 3.2 Managerial competences

people that fill it. Some business people see the key role as hiring and firing while others would more comprehensively include some or all of the following:

- establishing what work needs to be done and getting the right people with the right skills, who are appropriately rewarded;
- negotiating terms and conditions and monitoring attendance, performance, perhaps also progress;
- counter-balancing unions;
- lifting the skill base by providing appropriate training;
- advising on the most appropriate organisation.

Many personnel functions today also have a thirst for information which is often translated into a large number of forms that need to be correctly completed.

A narrow view of the personnel function seriously diminishes its potential, positive impact on the business. Of course, at business unit or factory levels there is a need to do bread-and-butter tasks. However, the key contributions where real value can be added are different:

1. *Management development*   the stock of managers must be enhanced in experiences and abilities, especially those who are on a fast track.
2. *Succession planning*   ensuring the right cover is in place and that the right development plans prepare people in the right way.
3. *Strategic thinking and strategy action plans*   high level input to forward plans that reflect the core personnel capability. This, of course, will reflect the world of change, and will not only influence staff practices or expectations but will also be reflected in organisational changes needed to deliver the strategy.

These three areas are the most important for quality input from personnel. The red-tape form-filling as their power base needs to be abandoned. Personnel executives must learn to have much greater influence without the support of form-based authority. The style of person needed is a change from the old stereotype hire-and-fire person. The new model must be a business person first, fully at ease with strategy, operations and key financial measures. While it may seem obvious that the human relations executive must have excellent interpersonal skills, these are regrettably missing in too many incumbents today.

Development of managers

Key processes to assist in the development of the managers are the following:

1. *Individuals*
   - objective setting;
   - appraisals;
   - career development reviews.
2. *Company or division*
   - management development plans;
   - succession planning.

The actual form of these documents is not very important except to recognise that in a large diverse company there is some merit in having a consistent approach but not at the expense of bureaucracy. A few practical comments on each of these areas follow.

Objective-setting

This is perhaps one of the first processes which will highlight a number of key items an individual needs to accomplish to make the contribution for which he or she will be accountable. The objectives need to be set in measurable terms where possible, with dates for achievement. If the focus is on those things for which the individual manager is accountable then it would be surprising if the list were longer than six or so key items. Based on the principle of linkage, the objectives will be based on the plans and budgets of the business unit where the manager is employed.

The objectives may well be refined during the year to take into account any new objectives which were not anticipated when objectives were originally set but which might arise during the year. For example, new objectives will arise on the acquisition of another company. Figure 3.3 shows how this takes place within the overall business process.

Strategic Plan

Budget

Objectives

Appraisal

Figure 3.3 Linking business and personnel processes

Appraisals

This is one of the most important interfaces between a manager and his or her direct reports (that is, those that report direct to the defined manager in an organisation). It is a two-way process based on the assessment of achievement against the agreed objectives. Personally, I like to see a self-appraisal written up and delivered to the direct report's manager before the appraisal meeting. However, the appraisor must be strong enough and sufficiently well-trained in the process to be proactive with his/her points and to discuss openly shortcomings or disagreements. The appraising managers need their own agenda, which will not be restricted to reactions to the self-appraisal. This debate is healthy stuff. The discussion is written up and signed off by both parties. The headings I have found most helpful as a focus for discussion are:

1. *Background* Brief description of outside factors that may have influenced performance including the need to deal with unexpected key events.
2. *Comments on objectives* Identifying the key achievements and those areas that were not fully achieved.
3. *Management development and team building* Although there will invariably be at least one key objective in this area, the focus on this most important aspect of management is very fruitful.
4. *Comments on overall performance* Because I believe that allocating a score to this area gives unhelpful bunching of average to above-average ratings and because this grading detracts from openness in the process, I prefer a word description. A paragraph can encapsulate the achievements much more appropriately.
5. *Comments on style and job competences* This is usually subjective but is very valuable. It enables the two people at the appraisal process to talk about interpersonal skills, qualities of leadership, allocation of time, personal attributes as well as addressing areas of competency for the specific role.
6. *Training and development plans* These will follow naturally from the discussion and will include specific areas of development. It also provides an opportunity to think of this topic more widely in the domain of the person being appraised.
7. *Career aspirations* Where a full career development review is appropriate – which certainly will not be annually or for each person – this is best done at another time. The reason for including it here is to look ahead five years, talk about the manager's aspirations, their realism, and to take on board their development implications.
8. *Additional items* This catch-all gives an opportunity for either party to raise quite naturally any other issue.

Career development reviews

These can be at the behest of the manager or the direct report. They are important when major changes are foreseen. It may be that a young manager wishes to move into general management or internationally from a local functional post. This ambition needs to be tested for realism. How does this sit against strengths and weaknesses or against the job description for the envisaged role? If the aspiration is realistic, what do both parties need to do to prepare the manager and over what time frame?

Management development and succession planning

This will be done annually first at the division or individual company level then at the corporate level to give the Board a bird's-eye view of the talent in the company. Once again, the actual form in which this is accomplished is less important than covering the right areas. The overall process covering the major areas of importance are shown diagrammatically in Figure 3.4. The process chosen will need to deliver an action statement which addresses key issues of top management whether they be in a large corporation or in an individual business unit. The key questions are:

1. What is happening in the outside world that will have a profound influence on the personnel plans? Legislation in Europe, changes in attitudes to employment, availability of graduates or demographic factors.
2. What changes to the quantity and quality of our people resource are needed to support the strategic plan? There may be special skills needed such as information technology capability. The plan may call for international initiatives that will have implications for management.
3. What are we doing about peaked managers, especially those that are blockages in the organisation?
4. Have we appropriately identified the cadre of high flyers and young managers of potential? There is a need to develop them and provide appropriate new demanding roles for them.
5. What are the succession issues? Does the company have cross-divisional or geographic moves planned for key people? Will there be cover in an emergency for top jobs? Will there be cover for a more natural succession timing?

It is fundamental for the organisation to question how it identifies managers of real potential or those currently with specific functions, who wish to go to general management. Finding the talent is about ensuring the future health of the business.

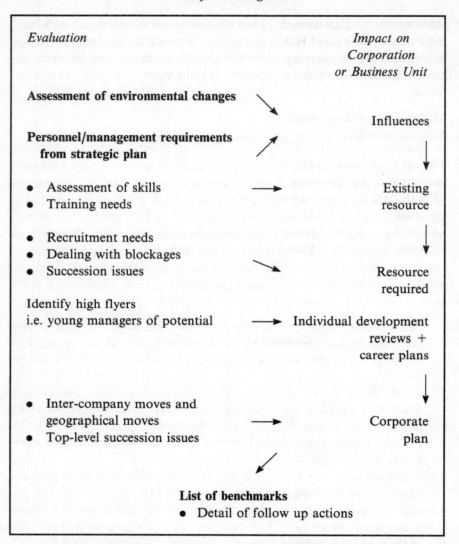

Figure 3.4 Management development: succession planning process

Finding the talent

There is still a great deal of subjectivity of trial and error in many companies as they try to seek out the top talent. The worldwide survey of senior business people shows that reliance on the past track record is a key factor. Has the manager proposed challenging objectives and achieved them? Can we deduce anything about leadership qualities from their past experiences? Has the manager shown a high degree of energy and enthusiasm in carrying out his roles? These are all valid pointers but are not alone likely to give uniformly good results.

Model of executive potential

In an endeavour to simplify the thought process yet maintain a degree of objectivity, I use a mental model as a base for assessment involving past performance and potential. There are, of course, a number of dimensions to both past performance and to potential which we need to assess in a systematic way, possibly involving some tests or Assessment Centres. Leadership is a key ingredient in both past performance and especially in assessing potential. Figure 3.5 illustrates the model.

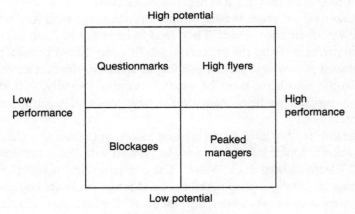

Figure 3.5 Executive potential

In Figure 3.5 *questionmarks* are the products of low performance yet they are judged to have high potential. There may well be special training needs for these people or perhaps a motivational problem in their current role. I am mindful of many bright, enthusiastic people who join companies with the feeling that they can change the world, yet in the first three to five years' experience they become disillusioned and turned off. Companies need to get to the bottom of this and provide the leadership that continues to motivate. It is for this reason especially that managers should look empathetically at 'questionmarks' asking first why the organisation failed these people.

The *high flyers* in the north-eastern quadrant are the high performance, high potential people we all aim for and who should be developed quickly and given some early chances to do jobs which will really stretch them. Perhaps some risk-taking is appropriate with this group by being prepared to promote them to a new role a shade too soon. It is surprising how quickly really good talent closes the gap between what is required for the job and the current level of capability.

Peaked managers are those with high current performance but with little potential to go beyond this job. These are the base level of managers who are doing a thoroughly worthwhile job but will not go further. Lateral shifts may be possible to refresh the manager. Equally, this group needs to receive training in new areas and to continue to be motivated to the goals of the organisation. It may well be that some of these managers are approaching retirement age so that new development posts are more likely to be given to managers of potential. Peaked managers need to be watched to ensure they do not become blockages.

Blockages in the south-western quadrant are those with low potential and a low performance record. They need to be removed from the current role, and probably from the organisation. This should not be a surprise as the appraisal process will have made this abundantly clear on an objective basis. People who leave must be treated straightforwardly, with dignity, and with support to help them find a new role and with appropriate payment.

Leadership is very hard to define and assess, yet it is a key element an organisation is looking for. I am very impressed with the achievements of General Electric under Jack Welch. The company devotes real effort to developing its total people capability – and it shows. In its endeavour to look systematically at leadership General Electric has developed a leadership assessment method which is comprehensive as well as valuable. It was included in the July/August 1993 issue of *The Chief Executive* magazine and covers an assessment by the boss, peers, subordinates and others. It would also be valuable to compare these assessments with the self-assessment which may also give a view about self-awareness. The approach is shown in Figure 3.6.

Saville & Holdsworth Limited, occupational psychologists, advise many organisations on selection of appropriate people for described roles. They also help companies to identify managers of potential or those suited for general management posts. They argue that the future is clearly not a replica of the past either in terms of requirements for success or the operating environment. Therefore, it is more appropriate to simulate key events likely to occur in the future. Tests can mimic events expected in the

Figure 3.6

Characteristic	Performance Criteria	Score
Vision	Has developed and communicated a clear, simple, customer-focused direction for the organisation.	
	Forward-thinking, stretches horizons, challenges imaginations.	
	Inspires and energises others to commit to Vision. Captures minds. Leads by example.	
	As appropriate, updates Vision to reflect constant and accelerating change impacting the business.	
Customer/ Quality Focus	Listens to customer and assigns the highest priority to customer satisfaction, including internal customers.	
	Inspires and demonstrates a passion for excellence in every aspect of work.	
	Strives to fulfil commitment to quality in total product/service offering.	
	Lives customer service and creates service mind-set throughout organisation.	
Integrity	Maintains unequivocal commitment to honesty/truth in every facet of behaviour.	
	Follows through on commitments; assumes responsibility for own mistakes.	
	Practises absolute conformance with company policies embodying the company's commitment to ethical conduct.	
	Actions and behaviours are consistent with words. Absolutely trusted by others.	
Accountability/ Commitment	Sets and meets aggressive commitments to achieve business objectives.	
	Demonstrates courage/self-confidence to stand up for beliefs, ideas, co-workers.	
	Fair and compassionate yet willing to make difficult decisions.	
	Demonstrates uncompromising responsibility for preventing harm to the environment.	
Communication/ Influence	Communicates in open, candid, clear, complete and consistent manner – invites response/ dissent.	
	Listens effectively and probes for new ideas.	

Figure 3.6 continued overleaf

Figure 3.6 continued

Characteristic	Performance Criteria	Score
Communication/ Influence	Uses facts and rational arguments to influence and persuade.	
	Breaks down barriers and develops influential relationships across teams, functions and layers.	
Shared Ownership/ Boundaryless	Self-confidence to share information across traditional boundaries and be open to new ideas.	
	Encourages/promotes shared ownership for team vision and goals.	
	Trusts others; encourages risk-taking and boundaryless behaviour.	
	Champions work-out as a vehicle for everyone to be heard. Open to ideas from anywhere.	
Team Builder/ Empowerment	Selects talented people; provides coaching and feedback to develop team members to fullest potential.	
	Delegates whole tasks; empowers team to maximise effectiveness. Is personally a team player.	
	Recognises and rewards achievement. Creates positive/enjoyable work environment.	
	Fully utilises diversity of team members (cultural, race, gender) to achieve business success.	
Knowledge/ Expertise/ Intellect	Possesses and readily shares functional/ technical knowledge and experts. Constant interest in learning.	
	Demonstrates broad business knowledge/ perspective with cross-functional/multicultural awareness.	
	Makes good decisions with limited data. Applies intellect to the fullest.	
	Quickly sorts relevant from irrelevant information, grasps essentials of complex issues and initiates action.	
Initiative/Speed	Creates real and positive change. Sees change as an opportunity.	
	Anticipates problems and initiates new and better ways of doing things.	
	Hates/avoids/eliminates 'bureaucracy' and strives for brevity, simplicity, clarity.	
	Understands and uses speed as a competitive advantage.	

Characteristic	Performance Criteria	Score
Global Mind-set	Demonstrates global awareness/sensitivity and is comfortable building diverse/global teams.	
	Values and promotes full utilisation of global and workforce diversity.	
	Considers the global consequences of every decision. Proactively seeks global knowledge.	
	Treats everyone with dignity, trust and respect.	

RATING SCALE: significant development need 1 2 3 4 5 outstanding strength.

Adapted with permission from *Chief Executive* magazine.

Figure 3.6   General Electric's leadership assessment (rated by manager, peers, subordinates)

future and assessment centres are a very valuable way of achieving some depth in this analysis. Saville & Holdsworth see the chances of identifying the right managers for a prescribed different role as 15 per cent if total reliance is placed on track record alone, rising to 35 per cent if there is a solid appraisal interview process with relevant checking of facts through appropriate third parties, but increasing to 75 per cent where assessment centres are also used. This, they claim, is also the order of magnitude of others like the American corporation AT&T who reviewed their success rate over a five-year period. This is a valuable aid but managers will be quick to appreciate that this is only a way of providing a more complete picture of candidates. It does not replace judgement which is critical in the selection process.

It is a key responsibility of management to find, develop, retain and motivate talented people. To achieve this goal the manager will need to make an investment of time and gain a deep knowledge of key people in their own work setting. This process demands real individual effort as well as support from personnel processes. There is also a need to have quality input from a capable personnel resource of a high calibre that is appropriate to the business demands of today and tomorrow.

What about the worker?

Management does not have the monopoly on good ideas, as we all know. Management literature, as well as living examples from today's companies, highlights many occasions when the workforce contributed towards superior performance. It is no longer acceptable to expect workers to check their brains in at reception before starting work. There is a large resource waiting to be tapped. We know that workers who feel involved can contribute more. It is also clear that where workers are given freedom to make their own decisions or to work as teams, quality and productivity increase. Jaeger Holdings Limited was one of the first companies to establish quick response production units as part of a team-working exercise. Instead of the repetitive processes which were broken down into as many as 100 operations with each operator performing in one specialised area, teams were created that set their own work plan. These teams were multi-skilled so that they would manage a complete garment. They were responsible for quality, output and the way they produced the garment. Clearly, there was much more job interest and work in progress was reduced to a day or so from the three weeks of the old 'bundle' system. Under team-working, benefits of higher productivity, fewer rejects and quicker turnaround of new garment designs were achieved with the reduction of working capital.

The way that individual managers involve the workforce will vary according to the company. However, there are some principles that will help with the process.

First, remember the power of communication and recall that it is a two-way process! Although this takes time and costs some money, it is a worthwhile investment. Frequency of contact is important as management cannot communicate only when they want something or if they try to use this as a chance to soften up the workforce before pay negotiations. Team briefings are an important element and should take place regularly according to the needs of the business, say, quarterly or monthly in some cases. Personally, I welcome the voluntary agreements which a number of forward-thinking British companies are making to form company-wide European Works Councils. They will provide opportunity for communication and discussion which is valuable and well worth the investment of top management time.

Second, make sure that the workforce is aware of the key elements of strategy, especially at the business unit level where they are employed. The implications of that strategy should be made known, especially areas of implication for labour.

Third, find ways to involve the workforce to help improve performance. Suggestion schemes through to working in specific task-focused teams with managers are all good ways to involve the workers.

Fourth, provide the opportunity for the workforce to improve their skills. There are plenty of options. Visits by selected people to other similar companies, to benchmark and learn, often provide a strong stimulus. In some cases, specialist workers can provide temporary help in another plant, sometimes overseas, and grow in skills as a result of this process.

Fifth, there are a multitude of in-house or external training schemes that provide for effective learning. These will range from very specialist areas to 'Investors in People', National Vocational Qualifications or quality initiatives such as ISO9000 or BS5050. There are also plenty of capable training firms who will help to supplement the in-house resource to add to the knowledge base of the workforce.

In summary, the workforce is a significant area of latent potential which is often under-utilised. When this is remedied, companies will improve their performance quite materially. The concept is relatively easy but it will take thought, effort and time to put it to work for the firm.

On a wider front, an organisation that is skilled at creating or acquiring knowledge and of setting up ways by which it can be transferred without distortion amongst its members will have a winning edge. Knowledge must lead to action so that behaviour is modified, is continuously monitored and adjusted according to the feedback. Talent is a key differentiator amongst companies today and it will be even more so in the future. This means that people must be placed before all else if the corporation is to gain true competitive advantage. Clearly, the rewards are longer term ones, as is the time frame one is influencing.

More to do

There are very important contributions to be made by commercially aware personnel professionals and some key processes that are helpful to improve the stock of talent. It is easy to be hampered by forms and red tape in this process yet this adds nothing. The effective input from personnel is through understanding and exerting influence in the organisation to help as part of the change process.

More work needs to be put into the process of identifying, recruiting, developing and retaining top people to fill the key roles. Call them high flyers if you like, but ensure that they are known by key senior managers and developed broadly. We need to also think if we have the balance of skills right with our key managers or those recruited from business schools. Think of the relative importance and the contrast between the following:

sequential thinking	vs	lateral thinking
corporate man	vs	entrepreneur
narrow and deep	vs	broad and aware
management technique	vs	leadership skills
energy and drive	vs	not rocking the boat

Personal development

The old adage that if we wish to be successful managers, then we should try managing ourselves is an important truism. In a business setting where learning is recognised as a core activity, managers need to ensure that they continue to grow and develop no matter how senior they are. Most would support this view as, like motherhood, it is judged to be worthy in its own right. Perhaps it is surprising that the managers surveyed (see Chapter 1) spend very little time on self-development. Only around 5 per cent of time was allocated for this purpose from a sample of successful general managers who rate self-development as important. Further down organisations, middle managers often complain that their company has done very little for them in providing structured learning opportunities.

Contrasting with this view, the more enlightened companies do have an amalgam of in-house courses perhaps held in conjunction with Business Schools, as well as specific external courses. During the appraisal process, the managers in these companies will pursue personal growth and training needs as a regular item. However, the quality of thinking by the appraiser and the personnel department is often lacking in providing appropriate training. It is hard work searching out hand-tailored solutions to individual training needs. Unfortunately there is no satisfactory substitute for this hard work, as a second-best solution simply to fill in an action point on their personnel record is not acceptable.

Even in the very best companies personal development and career planning must be the prime responsibility of the individual. This is far too important to be left to the company. Managers must be proactive about their careers, both in planning for the next step, as well as the preparation to achieve it.

The best managers have a really good, objective insight into themselves, knowing their preferred style of working, strengths and weaknesses. They will be aware of the fact that as they build their career, they will be building differing experiences to provide breadth as well as depth in preferred areas. Those working towards a goal of general management will have built up a variety of experiences often involving lateral moves as part of their development. Realism in goal-setting is important. For my part during my career, I have never set a goal beyond five years ahead and seldom for more than one significant step beyond the current role.

Setting personal objectives is in my view a productive activity. It clarifies the mind as to what is important, on the balance between differing goals related to family life, business, and wider aspirations. Having set personal goals managers need to order their lives to achieve these including the training and preparation that will best fit them for success. As we will see in Chapter 4, it is both possible and desirable to take a structured approach that will help to stimulate thinking towards managing one's own career development. The approach starts with a goal, moves into a self-appraisal of skills, looks at opportunities inside and outside the firm and ends up with an action programme.

Key messages

Management development is at the heart of successful organisations and it must be a key dimension of successful managers. Almost without exception managers today under-allocate time and resource here, in part because it is a difficult area, and in part because it can, in the short run, be avoided. This is an area that is important because it can create true competitive advantage.

Companies need to place management development, succession planning and the development of high flyers, further up the agenda for attention as well as resource. This will determine the future capability of the company, and may be the most significant way in which a successful manager can add greatest value.

Just as competent managers devote time to thinking about their company and how to deliver value, so too can they think about their personal objectives, and their own personal development plan. This, too, can be approached in a structured way, initiated by the manager and implemented with the understanding and support of his boss. The road to improvement starts out with self-improvement.

4 Managing Yourself

Life plan

One of the cardinal rules of good management is to understand how to manage *yourself*. This is a broader task than simply curbing the excesses of your temperament during difficult and trying times! It encompasses how you set your objectives, how you allocate your time, monitor your progress and how you relate to others. To put this into a wider setting each manager needs to see self-management within the wider context of a life plan that will be individual and perhaps personal to the author. This is not dissimilar from a business plan for a company, because it will start with goals (a mission) and will build a pathway from today to achieve these goals. I think that the wider setting of life goals is a valuable setting within which one of the important areas will be career planning. The goals need to be realistic, based upon an objective evaluation of one's own strengths and weaknesses.

Each successful manager will usually have a 'life plan'. Some will be explicit, clearly written down with milestones to achieve on their journey to the ultimate goal which is likely to be five years forward. Other plans will be less formal and may not be so carefully thought through. While the style will depend upon the individual, in my experience, the plans that are most effective are those that are more explicit.

There are different approaches to producing a life plan of course but I favour the simple approach which will have a number of key elements to it. As an optional first step it might be helpful to have some general long-term philosophical statement of where you would like to be towards the end of your lifetime. This is close to a mission statement for an individual business and sets the scene for the more specific medium-term goals. Second, set down those elements of life that are important to you and where you wish to set out some goals. This list is likely to cover:

- your career;
- your personal relationships including family;
- material things such as wealth, earnings, housing;
- personal development goals;
- other important areas such as spiritual, sport, outside interests, community involvement.

The best time frame is probably three to five years hence for this more specific list because it is usually unrealistic to plan beyond this period.

In Figure 4.1 an abbreviated plan for a young graduate in her mid-twenties who is currently working for a large strategic consulting company sets out her priorities and, importantly, is followed with the action plan needed to achieve these goals.

Avoid wishful thinking

If there is to be real value in such an exercise the starting-point must be based on an objective assessment of the manager's strengths and weaknesses. Equally, the goals must be realistic in the time frame and not based on wishful thinking. Successful managers have stretching but achievable goals and this area of life planning should be no exception. This is often a fruitful area to get some external input from a trusted friend or a mentor or to glean some from peers. Certainly, the feedback from a good appraisal system is valuable and any training needs identified in this process will have been followed up. Many managers find it of value to have an up-to-date profile of themselves based on preferences and straightforward psychometric tests. This not only aids self-awareness but will also help in understanding how to be more effective with interpersonal skills. Different styles of management interact in different ways and it is good to have a clear understanding of positive and negative attributes of those styles.

Measure progress

Once the goals have been set down regular reviews of progress towards them are important. I find the best time to do this is half-yearly, just prior to any review of objectives with the boss. Naturally, the annual review will be more comprehensive. Assuming that the plan covers three years, it is not necessary to rewrite such a document annually. However, a note of amendments to goals is a useful discipline to incorporate.

There will be a number of readers who may feel that it is unnecessary or even wasteful of time to adopt a written, more formal approach such as the one suggested here. Some suggest a more casual approach. The methodology is not the important issue. What is important is finding a disciplined way that will work for you. However, in my experience, the

Figure 4.1

Goals

Overall statement
I want to combine a successful career in industry with a family life. I want children, upper quartile income and a challenging career, probably in general management. I want to maintain my links with my church and serve the community through church charitable outlets.

Career
1. Within two years join an appropriate business firm to start building an industrial career. The entry is likely to be through the personnel or strategic planning functions.
2. Within five years to be a senior executive (just below board level) of a large FTSE 250 company or at board level of a smaller one.

Personal relationships
1. Strengthen relationship and commitments with John.
2. Marriage within five years (subject to continuing growth of relationship and mutuality with John).
3. Defer children until early 30s.

Material things
1. Double present salary to £60 000 in five years (in today's money values!)
2. Purchase a house with John – prefer London but this is not essential.

Personal development
1. Need to build better interpersonal skills.
2. Need to develop leadership and skills in managing subordinates.
3. Need to free more time from work activities to get a better balance in life.

Other areas
1. Maintain physical fitness through twice a week visits to gym and once a week at badminton club.
2. Maintain current level of involvement in church, especially the help to the elderly in our area.

Action plans
1. Talk with John about goals (in broad terms first!)
2. Search for new career opportunities;
   - build links with search firms within 12 months
   - identify better companies that may be of interest within 12 months.
3. Arrange external courses on aspects of leadership and managing people soonest.
4. Decide within the next 12 months if an MBA programme is a preferred optional route. If so, which university and consider part time versus full time.

Review of progress
Note: This is completed later – updated with progress made and showing any amendments to goals that might transpire through the time period.

Figure 4.1 Life plan – Sarah Jones

quality of thinking that goes into the more formal method is greater, and the commitment to goals is certainly higher when these are written down. In the course of 12 months or so, goals that were not formalised may well be varied or even forgotten. The approach outlined here has certainly worked for me and, with some variations, has worked well for many successful managers.

Personal career plan

Some managers prefer a formal plan to focus solely on personal career planning. Indeed, this view is supported by the processes within a company. When a manager wishes to discuss his/her career plan with the company he/she will usually prepare fairly formally for this. A suggested approach is shown in Figure 4.2 which follows a standard pattern of logic:

1. setting out objectives;
2. recognising the key qualities needed to achieve the goal;
3. recognising from an objective assessment of skills where improved knowledge or performance is needed;
4. a clear pattern of actions that will help to reach to the goal.

The final step of persuading the boss, as well as the personnel department, to agree these objectives and series of actions is critical to the success of the career plan.

---

1. My career objectives are:
   (list objectives with realistic milestones and dates to achieve these)

2. What are the key personal qualities needed to achieve these goals, and what progress am I making to optimise these? For example

   - Specific areas of business knowledge
   - Interpersonal skills
   - Ability to communicate
   - Knowledge of the industry – the firm
   - Intellectual capacity, conceptual thinking
   - Varied practical experiences
   - Integrity and reputation
   - Judgement
   - Others relevant to goal

3. What is the really key area of improvement or knowledge enhancement needed given the assessment above?

4. What are the realistic opportunities that may become available in the near future within the firm? Am I seen to be a clear candidate?

5. Given my objectives and an objective appraisal of strengths and weaknesses, what training programmes or experiences do I need to undertake to be a preferred candidate?

6. Action list
   Ensure that my boss endorses this list and commits equally to it. Action steps follow.

   Step 1   **Date**
   etc.   etc.

Figure 4.2 Personal career planning

Self-knowledge

Successful managers really understand themselves. They are fully aware of their preferred style, of strengths and weaknesses and those that best supplement them to make an effective team. Any manager preparing a life plan must start with the present position. The manager must answer the question objectively 'Where am I now?'. For those working within a business firm, they will readily identify the multifaceted nature of this task. As an illustration, Figure 4.3 suggests some useful headings for a manager's self-assessment.

---

1. What is my preferred style of working?
   - What are the positive aspects of this?
   - What are the negatives?
   - What actions do I need to take?

2. What is my level of knowledge of basic facts?
   - the industry
   - the firm
   - products
   - processes
   - customers
   - competitors

3. What is my level of understanding of external factors that influence my current role?

4. What is my level of professional knowledge?
   - How do I rate against peers?
   - How up to date am I?

5. What real progress in personal learning and development have I made in the past 12 months? (Give specific examples.)

6. How are my relations with others?
   - superiors
   - subordinates
   - peers
   - through networks

Figure 4.3 Manager's self-assessment

capable-idol

There are many examples of managers who are apparently capably carrying out their responsibility but who suffer from a blind spot about their style, strengths or weaknesses. It is for this reason that a number of companies include, as part of their management development plans, an opportunity for managers' self-assessments to be compared with the evaluations of superiors, subordinates and peers. Included in Chapter 3 is a practical example from General Electric (see Figure 3.6). At London Business School, Professor John Hunt routinely conducts such analysis for specialist company courses run for their partnership companies. Managers rate this feedback and this insight as the most valuable session of an excellent, high-level programme.

As part of the original survey outlined in Chapter 1, the case of Anton, a senior marketing director from a fast-moving consumer goods company, was raised in discussions with successful managers. His case is far from unusual. His self-perception was remarkably different from how others saw him. Case Study 4.1 summarises his career and the key lessons that were drawn from this.

Stages in career

The plans towards goals and the emphasis of managers' fundamental initiatives will vary according to the level they have reached and the stage in their life. John Kotter, in his book *Power and Influence*, talks of three stages. He sees the early career as the first stage where the key role of the manager is to develop an adequate power base. The second stage is in mid-career where the emphasis is on using power without abusing it. The third and final stage is in late career and is all about letting go gracefully.

This is a useful framework against which to look at the expectations within a role at different stages in the work life-cycle. The idea of a life-cycle prompted me to think more in terms of stages of life which I have summarised in Figure 4.4.

Early in the career is a sensitive time both for the new employee and for the company. At the time of first appointment it is rare that the new recruits have a clear view of what they will realistically want from a business career. They may well have naïve expectations founded on altruism or an incomplete knowledge of themselves. This is a vulnerable period when the company needs to provide large doses of help and advice. A good mentor will assist to guide relationship patterns of learning and to gain broad experiences that will become a useful foundation for good future performance.

──────────────── **Case Study 4.1** ────────────────

Understanding oneself

Anton was the Marketing Director of a fast-moving consumer goods company (FMCG) in South Africa. He had been in the role for more than five years having been promoted through the ranks as brand manager for several major product groups. Prior to this, he had spent seven years in an advertising agency, mostly as a copy-writer where his wit, caustic style of writing and zany humour was given free reign. He was promoted to account management but this was less than totally successful because his unusual style was not universally accepted by his clients. However, he saw an opportunity to join one of the client companies to extend his experience and begin a commercial career. This is how he came to be with FMCG.

During his time with the company, he had been promoted at varying stages of his career within marketing to become Marketing Director at the age of 42 years. He had also, earlier in his career, experienced a short spell as a sales supervisor. Two years later, the Chief Executive decided to combine sales and marketing on the retirement of the Sales Director. Anton was appointed because of his good relationship with the advertising agency that continued to produce highly creative work and because he seemed to get on well with the sales force who loved his presentations and joking style. It was also noted that he had direct sales experience.

One aspect of Anton's performance as Sales and Marketing Director which concerned the company's Chief Executive was the high staff turnover in marketing as well as Anton's inability to meet timetables. His direct reports were loyal to him but highly frustrated with his interfering, driving style and his continual need to take all decisions himself. His staff did not grow in their jobs and most would leave within two or three years.

During appraisal time Anton was finally confronted with this area of weakness. His boss saw him as creative but incapable of offering leadership and developing his team. Failure to meet deadlines was caused by his apparent inability to delegate. This was very different from Anton's own evaluation. He saw himself as highly creative with high leadership skills, who motivated and developed his team to a stage where they were quickly snapped up by other employers who recognised the training they had received. He also openly talked of his aspirations to succeed the Chief Executive in two years when he retired.

To resolve these issues it was decided to profile Anton getting input from his subordinates and peers and to contrast this with his own self-perception. The two views were poles apart.

Anton's self-perception	*Third parties' consensus*
● Highly creative	● Eccentric, different, likeable, socially gregarious
● Extrovert, good with people	● Poor man manager, will not delegate
● Excellent leader	● Confusion all around, no goals or benchmarks
● Builds teams	● Direct reports do not grow. No responsibility given, staff are progressors or administrators.
● Good grasp of commercial issues.	● No understanding of the wider business imperatives.

When confronted with this analysis, Anton was devastated, lost confidence and his performance fell off further. It was now clear to him that general management was an unrealistic career goal. He applied for and received a transfer to the subsidiary company in the United States as Marketing Director of a division which was young and growing. He was supported with good administration and had been counselled on areas of weakness. Within 18 months he left the company as he was seen to be unsuccessful in the new environment which was his first foreign posting and for which he had been poorly prepared. He was lost without the creative input of the agency that had served him so well in South Africa.

Key Lessons

1. Clear self insight and knowledge of strengths and weaknesses is essential in any manager.
2. The appraisal process should have identified the areas requiring modified behaviour or improvement early.
3. Career-development counselling would have immediately ruled out general management at an earlier date.
4. A foreign posting of a 'problem child' employee gives a very low chance of success. The first golden rule of good management development programme is that only the very best talent gets cross-boundary postings. Never 'export' problem children.

Stages of awareness during Development.

Stage	Activities, drivers	Pressures
1. Adolescence (3–5 years experience) *unconscious incompetence*	• Learning • Sponge-like, soak up information • Understanding self – who am I? • Build relationships • Gain acceptance • Get noticed – put runs on the board.	• Distractions – next tangerine • Disillusioned – mature Welcomes to Cheerapan? • Naïvety may turn to cynicism
2. Young adulthood (up to 10 years experience) *conscious incompetence*	• Need for achievement • Progress must be visible • Material gains	• Partner's goals • Balance with external goals • Family begins?
3. Middle Age (10–30 years experience) *conscious competence*	• Responsible, in control • Long-run and short-term goals • Maturity	• Work time demands versus other claims. • Provide for family needs, e.g. education and emotional support. • Support partner's career (often new)
4. Elder, greying guru (25–40 years experience) *unconscious competence*	• Statesman • Source of wisdom • Big picture • Leave an appropriate 'monument' • Find successor	• Ambivalence over letting go. • Need to develop new interests. • How best to contribute to community. • Need 'to be wanted'

Figure 4.4 Four stages of management

In the period of 'young adulthood' the manager will certainly have taken on the first position of significant responsibility and made the first substantial step towards the five-year goals. As the potential age range of managers is likely to be between 25 years of age and perhaps 35 years of age there will also be a need for balance. This may be occasioned by a partner's goals which will be recognised as perhaps the beginning of family responsibility.

The broadest span of time is the one of mid-career or middle age in my life analogy. Responsibilities at work are large, time commitments and travel are often significant while, at the same time, family needs, both emotional and financial, are high. While this is a time of change, often between different roles, it is frequently a time when emotional strength is tested. In many cases work pressures are coupled with severe family pressures which will test and sometimes result in the breakdown of relationships.

Finally, the elder greying guru who is the source of much wisdom and whose prime aim is to pick a successor. Here, an ambivalence of giving up and not letting go will be common. It is also a time when managers will want to contribute more both to society and, through the managers' experiences, to younger people in the organisation. This is an excellent time to use such managers as mentors.

Management of time

Professor Northcote Parkinson observes as one of his famous Parkinson Laws that 'work expands to fill up the time available'. This is often true and we all have examples of managers who work longer than required hours simply because they have allowed work to fill up space that was previously free. Again, there are examples of managers who believe that a high level of activity is compatible with performance as a manager. As an example of the latter case, Allan, a manager with a long period of international experience in a drinks company, was perpetually on the move, visiting every market frequently in a frenzy of activity. He was personable, sociable and good with the distributors. The trouble was that he was not a thinker, did not deal with priorities of different markets by radically changing distribution arrangements in some non-performers and he did not have a development plan for those with growth prospects. The system protected him because each year his budget was largely achieved and his results showed incremental growth. He seldom wrote reports; he was only infrequently in the office of his headquarters.

A new chief executive replaced Allan within the first six months of his appointment because he recognised that the days of the travelling public relations man were past and that Allan was not able to learn marketing and thinking skills or to change his work style significantly. This was a failure of the company first and of the manager second.

Priorities

Every manager with a challenging job will find that time management is an essential part of efficiency. Depending upon his/her level within the organisation, a manager will have a greater or less ability to manage personal time. Most successful managers will have a system or an approach that works for them and which will be understood and respected by superiors, peers and subordinates. It requires the making of a list as follows:

1. What are the things I must do?
2. What are the things I should do as soon as time permits?
3. What are the things I would like to do?

Depending on the nature of the manager's job, there will also be a time facet:

1. The big picture – what are the really significant things that will make a big difference to the value added in my current role?
2. Take a week at a time:
   - what must I do?
   - what should I do?
   - what would I like to do?
3. Take a day at a time:
   - what must I do?
   - what should I do?
   - what would I like to do?

To be really effective as well as gaining some valuable insight, managers should keep a regular record of how they spend their time. If they are typical, they will be surprised how much time is spent 'fire-fighting' or responding to the needs of others. General managers in the survey were often surprised how little time they spent thinking about the future or preparing themselves and their staff through appropriate management development plans to lift performance significantly.

Allocate time for your priorities, negotiating if necessary with your boss on how you can be more efficient in achieving this. Make sure that within your allocation of time there is a chunk blocked out for what *you* want to do. Some high-quality, non-interrupted space is needed to think about the future or to think about the really big issues. Do not be too parsimonious with the time for this very special activity. You should aim for 15 per cent but not accept less than 10 per cent.

What works best for you?

Each manager will know the time when he/she is at his/her most creative or when high-quality thinking is easiest. These precious moments should be segmented off for higher-quality work. Each manager will choose a system that is easy and works well for them. There is nothing novel in how I manage my time. I know I am far better in the early morning than late at night and therefore try to free some morning times for thinking, for strategy and forward plans. My approach is broadly as follows:

1. I have a vision of where I want to see the company in the next five years. This is the very broad picture that has been communicated to the next level of management.
2. I have an agreed list of annual objectives which are compatible with the strategic plan. I expand these objectives to reflect the layering of objectives through to the next level, to my direct reports. I review progress against these objectives monthly, noting where we are falling behind milestones or key dates or changing these where circumstances appropriately dictate this.
3. I always have a current 'work book' with me. This is just a notebook where I record my week's key tasks divided into the three categories already mentioned. I then have a list of a dozen or so other important items that either I must, should, or would like to complete in the week. Incidentally, I use the right-hand side of this book to record key points from discussions or telephone calls. This is an invaluable prompt to action and destroys the fear of forgetting.
4. Every day I arrive at the London office early, usually prior to 7.30am. I read *The Financial Times*, having already read one other quality paper on the way to work. During the first half hour I plan out the day, noting especially key tasks from the week that must or should be done. I dislike being interrupted during this time.
5. From 8.00am onwards meetings can start or 'phone calls to Australia and the Far East can be made.

People in my office know my routine, respect it, but will interrupt me at any time if it is important. I prefer to have regular meetings with key people organised through my secretary to keep good order. Every successful manager knows that one of the greatest potential forces for their efficiency and effectiveness is an empowered, capable secretary. If your secretary does not fit that description then the probability is that you do not deserve someone that good!

The too-hard basket

There is a tendency in most managers to put off difficult or unpleasant tasks. I call this the 'too-hard basket' which is often the receptacle of many important projects that are left for a variety of reasons. The contributing factors often form a pattern which includes the following:

- The task requires input from a number of people and data is incomplete and difficult to get.
- The task is complex.
- A chunk of quality thinking time is needed but is never available.
- It is beyond the previous experience of the manager who has the responsibility to progress the issue.

Dealing with the 'too-hard basket' requires discipline and appropriate time and resource. There is no 'magic bullet' that gives an instantaneous solution but some things will help in these circumstances. Consider asking the following questions:

- What is the real reason why this is not being progressed?
- Is the task difficult through complexity or because the environment is changing rapidly, destroying precedents or points of reference?
- Is the task time-sensitive?
- Do I need help?
- Would a group meeting allocating responsibilities to get all of the relevant information help?
- Can the project be broken down into smaller, manageable chunks?

Managing your boss

We frequently read in the business press that incompatible chemistry between a boss and his subordinate leads to a replacement subordinate or certainly to a suboptimal relationship. Managing your boss is just about as important as managing your career. It has to be taken seriously and proactively by every direct report.

There are some rules that are helpful in managing your boss. First, you need to know how the boss's preferred style interacts with your own. This will warn of potential areas for clash, of ways that the boss will be irritated and how best to present ideas to him. Within my experience, where a boss and one of his managers always clashed both were helped by seeing the widely different styles and the impact upon each other.

Second, the manager needs to understand the agenda and objectives of the boss. This enables a 'win–win' situation where, with the understanding of the different styles, a manager must work at building on relationships. Trust is essential. It is difficult to build but can be lost quickly with unthinking actions.

Third, there is a need to communicate freely so that the 'no surprises' rule is maintained. There is not always a need for formal communication but including the boss in communications about your subordinates' achievements occasionally is usually appreciated. Equally, depending upon his style, the manager may prefer to tell the boss early in a project about the way it is going forward to avoid the prospect of rejection when the project is completed.

Good common sense is the key criterion here. The successful, self-confident manager will also not be afraid to ask the boss for advice or to talk through concepts before setting out on some new project. To involve the boss early on and make him or her part of the early thinking and planning often leads to better support when the project is ready for final presentation.

A review

Managing yourself is an essential prerequisite to becoming a successful manager. There is a systematic approach that will enhance your ability to be more effective and to get greater value from the time available. Reputation is the greatest asset of all in an executive and this is of course enhanced by the quality of his/her output, integrity and the perception of his/her track record. The key messages that emanate from this chapter are:

- There is great value in a manager having an overall life plan that has as a key element a career plan. Formal, written plans often work best.
- The building-up of interpersonal relationships at varying levels within and outside the business is a highly important activity.

- Really successful managers have a clear objective understanding of themselves, their preferred style of working, their strengths and weaknesses.
- Different stages of a management life-cycle are discernable and have their unique key drivers or primary activities as well as pressures which need to be recognised.
- The effective management of time is a potential differentiator of the very successful manager from those who are more pedestrian. A systematic individual approach will ensure that priorities are tackled in good time.
- The 'too-hard basket' is usually a figment of your mind and can be dealt with by setting priorities and through a recognised framework of action.
- Managing your boss is a key task for every manager. It requires knowledge of styles, of the agenda, as well as thoughtfulness and communication.

5   The Environment

Managers, look out

Managers need to 'look out' much more than they are accustomed to doing. For quite understandable reasons across the world, today's managers are focused on fixing urgent problems that demand attention *now* and have little time left to exercise their curiosity about outside trends and influences on the company. This is perfectly understandable given the pressures of flatter organisations, of pressure on the bottom line of profitability, and the focus on slashing costs in an organisation. It is just like the person sitting at home preparing a household budget for the year ahead which is seen as an important task given the pressure on the household finances. However, at the same time, the bath is running upstairs and given the preoccupation with budgets the bath is now overflowing with water coming down the stairs. While the task of budgeting is important, this must be left to attend to the urgent chore of turning off the water!

There are many business people today who unfortunately do not have time for anything other than the urgent! There is no doubt that the really successful managers are not just competent to do their jobs and are not just dealing with the 'urgent' tasks of the day with competence and skill. They will order their lives to find time for 'important' work too. The very best managers will be aware of trends and influences, deducing from their unique perspective in the company new, improved ways of adding shareholder value. Some do this intuitively, without effort, because their psychometric profile is like that. Others will need to find time and systematically work through a process to find influences that will impact on their business providing opportunity and threats. To help to illustrate the systematic approach, we will examine the broad environment which is an important initial step in the business model as a way of highlighting an important dimension of successful management.

Environment and the business model

No business firm exists in isolation. It has customers, competitors and suppliers and operates in the real world of change. It is subject to the influence of the broad economic and political forces that impact upon it, whether for the firm's advantage or disadvantage. There are external trends that at worst will be ignored to cause irreparable damage and at best will lead to serious suboptimisation of business performance. These are the main reasons why we need to consider the environment seriously.

It is useful to think systematically about the environment and how it might change in the future to try to find trends that will impact on the theatre in which the business operates. If trends can be spotted early they can be exploited as a source of competitive advantage, or where they may impact negatively then corrective action can be taken in good time.

In this chapter we shall examine how it is possible to look methodically at the outside environment, perhaps to find evidence of significant change that should be taken into account in future strategies or action plans. To give a simple illustration, there are many companies in the United Kingdom that in the 1980s put down significant production investment in sophisticated production plants that give the opportunity of 24-hour working and producing at a lower cost to match that of their continental rivals. These large plants were costly, required long production runs of standardised products and gave the prize of lower costs. The trade-off was a lack of flexibility and just as many plants were coming on-stream, the trend for greater customisation was increasingly obvious. Consumers were demanding individuality, a degree of customisation and significant variety as well as value for money.

With the benefit of hindsight, the trend was clear before the decision to purchase the large specialised plants. The production executives were seduced by the prize of brand new 'state of the art' plants yielding low cost as the reward and with the production function being much more powerful within the organisation. In some extreme cases, production would determine what would be made available for the consumer, both in product type as well as packaging. There are numerous examples that are well-known from the confectionery industry, the food industry and motor vehicles.

Some managers today remain so focused on their current, everyday task that they do not look outwards or try to deal with the imprecise, softer issues implicit in dealing with the environment. This is a quite natural reaction. However, there is clear evidence that the best managers are alert to wider issues and think how these will impact on the context of both the business and private arenas.

Business model

In order to set out the bigger picture it is worth briefly having a look at a model for business which is shown in Figure 5.1. This is a systematic approach that will assist managers to spot trends early and to put in place the competencies or unique skills that will help to achieve early delivery of the goals of the firm. This is then followed by an action plan. Typically, managers would undertake this exercise at the start of a strategic plan. The key focus in this chapter is on the environment which is the opening section of the model.

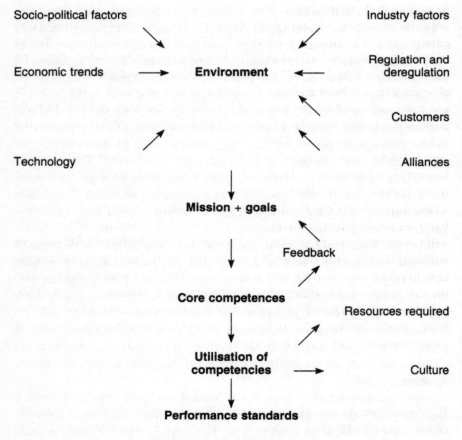

Figure 5.1 Model for business

Successful managers who are alert to trends and possibilities in the future will read widely about issues and ideas that seem at first blush to be peripheral to their main activities. Ian Pearson and Peter Cochrane of BT Laboratories have recently published a thought-provoking article '200 Futures for 2020'. In Figure 5.2 I have listed in an abridged form some of their key expectations. This approach is a useful starting-point for debate to try to distil those trends that might have impact on the business. Effectiveness is aided by focusing on broad headings such as socio-political factors, economic trends, technology, industry factors, regulations, customers and alliances. Let us have a brief look at each of these:

Socio-political facts

Searching the environment will cover a wide range of disciplines and areas of impact on the company. It will cover sociopolitical factors that emerge and will change over time. Shifts in expectations of different consumer groups and across geography can have a meaningful impact on the strategy that a firm will adopt. Also included here are demographic changes that will have an important influence on products or services that are being provided to the market-place. Does the relative ageing of the population in the Western world, for example, have implications for the industry or for the firm? The growing affluence of the grey consumers coupled with their increased leisure time does indeed have consequences for many organisations. How will industry attract, motivate and fully utilise a labour force that will inevitably be older in the next century? These implications need to be thoroughly thought through. On the other hand, in developing countries, there are different dynamics. More people will have discretionary purchasing power. The age profile will be younger with implications for purchasing power priorities. India is an interesting case in point. Its relatively very young population has a significant impact on the range of consumer goods and services a company offers. This, together with increasing purchasing power enabling consumers to move from 'needs' to 'wants', is having an important influence on purchasing power that differs from the Western world.

Economic trends

Economic trends are also of importance in trying to pull together a strategy that will give competitive advantage. An international firm knows that it must take a view about relative rates of growth of different

Figure 5.2

Biotechnology, health and medical
- New engineered organisms used to produce chemicals.
- Widespread genetic intervention programmes for plants and animals.
- Custom foods will exist for particular medical conditions.
- Genetic link of all diseases identified.
- Genetic screening widely used and genetic programmes to enhance human well-being.
- Full personal medical records stored on a smart card.
- Most people will live into their 80s in good health.
- Many synthetic body parts.
- Home-based health diagnostic systems.
- Devices roaming within blood vessels under their own power.
- Direct pleasure production.

Business
- Global electronic currency in use.
- Paper and coins largely replaced by electronic cash.
- Virtual companies dominant.
- Purely electronic companies exist – minimal human involvement.
- Universal monitoring of business transactions.

Education and the pursuit of knowledge
- Life-long learning is the norm.
- Distance learning widespread.
- Expert systems surpass human learning and logic abilities.
- Real-time language translation for print and voice.
- Broadband, networked, electronic libraries.
- Very intelligent pursuit of knowledge and consultation.
- Systems to understand text and drawings (e.g. patents).
- Subliminal learning.
- Machine use of human memorising, recognising, learning.

Energy
- Cost of energy will be higher.
- Cities and accommodation designed to be more efficient.
- Solar cells with efficiency > 30 per cent.
- Multi-layered solar cells with efficiency > 50 per cent.
- Common use of solar cells for residential power supply.
- Solar power stations in space.

Environment
- Totally managed world environment (includes industry, oceans, forests, etc.).

- More effective resource management.
- Effective intervention in natural disasters (to control effects).
- Widespread contamination by a nuclear device.
- Deep underground cities.
- Artificial precipitation induction.
- Global environmental management corporations.

In IT literacy
- Everyone in advanced nations computer-literate.
- IT literacy essential for any employment.

Machine input
- Highly integrated bio sensors.
- Speech dialling with recognition in switch equipment.
- Odour and flavour sensors that mimic humans.
- Machine recognition of body language and gestures.
- Bio-sensors capable of processing information.

Materials
- Atomic customisation of materials.
- Intelligent materials with sensors, storage and effectors.
- Smart skins for intelligent clothing and direct human repair.
- Use of polymer gels for muscles, bioreactors, information processing.
- Membranes with active transport and receptors.

Memory and storage
- Various examples of massive increases in capability and speed.

Processing
- Very widespread embedded intelligence.
- Extensive use of analog and neural processing.
- Technology imitating the thinking processes of the brain.
- Computers will write much of their own software.

Robotics
- Robots will be commonplace, e.g. in homes, factories, hospitals, building and construction, maintenance, security and entertainment.
- Domestic small robots will be specialised.
- Totally automated factories will be common.
- Intelligent robots for unmanned plants.
- Robots for guiding blind people.
- Autonomous robots with environmental awareness sensor.
- Self-diagnostic, self-repairing robots.

Figure 5.2 continued overleaf

Figure 5.2 continued

Security
- Universal ID Cards including a wide range of data.
- Crime and terrorism will be largely computer-based.
- Fire detection by odour or vibration.
- Fire-fighting robots that can find and rescue people.

Social
- Products of all kinds will be customised.
- Infrastructures will be self-monitoring.
- English will be the global language.
- On-line voting.
- Electronic shopping will be the norm for many products.
- World population > 7.5 billion.
- Migration regulated by international law.
- State pensions on a need-only basis (income-tested).
- More recreation and leisure time for middle classes.
- Mass starvation continues in the Third World.
- Rise of secular substitutes for religion, e.g. network-based groups.
- Electronic newspapers to households.
- Various forms of electronic addiction will be a big problem.
- Power will be held by corporations rather than by countries.

Space
- Orbiting space station well-developed.
- Regular manned missions to Mars.
- Space planes in practical use.
- Space factories for commercial production.
- Moon-base the size of a small village.

Transport
- Interactive vehicle highway systems.
- Use of fibre gyros in car navigation.
- Various traffic information systems in use, e.g. dynamic routing, monitoring taxation and crime prevention.
- Energy provided by hydrogen fuel cells and/or solar power.
- Nuclear propulsion for some forms of transport.
- Fully automatic ships able to navigate and dock automatically.
- Passenger planes with speeds of > mach four and > 300-seat capacity.
- Super conductive magnetic levitation railways at 500 miles per hour.

SOURCE: Abridged and adapted from Ian Pearson and Peter Cochrane, *BTs Futures Report*.

Figure 5.2 Futures for 2020

geographical areas as part of the input towards their strategy. Typically, China is noted for its size, its growth rate and future potential. This needs to be matched against the risks that are seen in the same time frame.

Technology

Technology is impacting more and more on the environment and in choices that managers need to make. The business model adopted by firms will need to reflect technology advances and decide how these will impact on the business. More importantly, managers will need to decide how competitive advantage can be created. Information technology (IT) is the first area usually recognised but not always embraced by general managers. Top management are beginning to recognise that advanced computing and communication tools are becoming an increasing part of life. However, there are other important areas such as biotechnology, the growing importance of the global electronic highways and the ability to use interactive multimedia.

Naturally enough, not all these broad areas will impact equally on the terrain of all firms or managers but it is helpful to have a screening process to evaluate each of them at least. Take for example, the less publicised area of biotechnology. Let us take a specific example to illustrate the scope of some trends. The European Union's 1993 White Paper on Growth, Competitiveness and Employment recognised this as a key area which needed to be harnessed if Europe is to develop and grow its economy. This was reinforced in the Commission's Report in September 1994 on 'An Industrial Competitiveness Policy for the EU'. While most observers would readily see the new trendy biotechnology companies that have mushroomed over the past few years, it is less clear that businessmen have recognised the impact on existing industries, processes and products.

Ernst and Young, who have surveyed this area, observe that biotechnology 'is revolutionising many sectors of industry'. To give some order of magnitude of the impact:

- Nearly 200 000 jobs in Europe depend on biotechnology and the growth rate of such employment will increase far faster than in other types of industry.
- Europe spends about £0.75 billion on R&D in this area while the USA spends considerably more. The bias in European expenditure is to find enabling capacity.

- The total European market for goods dependent on biotechnology is estimated at £30 billion. At least within Europe biotechnology is identified as an area of challenge, and its pervasiveness is far-reaching across Europe.

Not only do we see a wide array of science and technology touching almost every business, we also see the speed of change accelerating. For example, we confidently expect computers to double in performance in under two years and the costs of computing to decline fairly rapidly. There is seldom a need to accept any time lag between transactions and information, or indeed to have other than shared databases which can be freely interrogated.

For many industries, the impact of wireless communication will have an impact on their place of work in that access to information will remain easy wherever the worker is placed. Within supermarkets, electronic price tagging will give the ability to change prices effortlessly from a central point giving flexibility if desired to change prices, say during 'convenience hours' when the competition may be different from core shopping hours. New products such as personalised newspapers may be available, perhaps delivered electronically to home computers.

Industry factors

These are examples only of some of the broad macro-environmental trends that businesses may wish to address in their planning. Still dealing with the environment, there is a group of areas that are more related to the industry or the firm itself. A broad first sweep is of industry factors including competition. Do we understand in depth what the competition's goals, strategy and core capabilities really are? What have they done that has provided wins and where have they lost out? Are there new entrants and on what basis will they compete? What factors are changing that will affect the whole industry? For example, if speed of response and zero stock-holding by customers is becoming the norm, what does this imply for the industry?

Regulation

The same approach will apply to regulation which may well be increasing through the dead hand of European bureaucrats for example or deregulation of an industry as we have seen with airlines. Products currently produced in developing countries will increasingly transfer their production base to the lower cost, developing countries, where the labour costs are typically only 3 per cent of the average costs in Europe. Here, the benefit will be lower costs for sourced products with the challenge of getting quick response to avoid obsolete stock write-downs because of fashions changing. IT will have a part to play in achieving the desired speed of response. There may well be implications for high labour cost capacity in developed economies as more manufacturers move offshore to take advantage of lower cost labour.

Customer base

The customer base will deal not only with change in their needs but broad issues such as growing concentration, changes in channels of distribution or broad trends such as ecological concerns. To illustrate this, suppliers to the clothing retailers need to find new ways of taking time out of the supply chain to remove risk and improve retailers' efficiency of working capital. This may well require a shift in the supply base that improves speed of response, ability to communicate through IT and to provide value for money to the final user. As a second illustration, channels of distribution have been and are continuing to change away from the independents to the major retailers who are continuing to gain market share. Here, forward strategies will concentrate on providing a unique service package to these major customers that are tailor-made to their requirements. The partnership of supplier and customer will choose from the permutations available a package that meets the needs of the particular customer and which is commercially viable to the supplier. New channels of distribution will emerge so that retailers may wish to try out specific mail order opportunities or move more widely into TV sales channels like QVR or in the future consider direct home access through cabling and computers.

Customers' requirements are so vital to all business future developments yet too often they receive plenty of lip-service but very little true dialogue or understanding. However, many successful companies will regularly survey their customers to establish their future plans about their current and future expectations of the supplier and to receive an assessment of current relative performance. This is an important forward step. It can, however, also be misleading, as the firm conducting the survey misses out completely the views of potential customers. Companies may well learn more from lapsed customers or those who have not yet been recruited than they learn from interrogating the loyal customer base. Perhaps, more importantly, a firm's future customers which it serves in five to ten years time may well be very different from those it is serving today. Talking to customers is a very necessary factor for success.

Alliances

Increasingly, in a complex world, there will be alliances formed between suppliers and customers, manufacturers and their customers and even between competitors. These will be across geography and will allow collaboration to give groups of firms advantages of time, cost or capability. As an example, Rover's collaboration with Honda probably rescued British Leyland, or at least gave it a significant competitive advantage, while giving benefits of faster payback to Honda for their investment. It is ironical that the reward to Honda for their contribution to Rover's success was that British Aerospace sold Rover off to BMW so that the parent could focus on its core area of defence.

Pause to reflect

So far in this chapter two points have been made. First, really successful managers have an ability to absorb from the environment relevant trends that will impact on their business and on their personal life space. Managers will be outwardly aware and alert to significant external changes. This is not always easy because it requires time, thinking ability and good allocation of time. Really successful managers exercise their curiosity over a wide front, thinking about broad issues that do not always appear to be immediately relevant to their company. The breadth of the environmental scan can be seen, for example, in the work undertaken by the World Economic Forum which is headed by Professor Klaus Schwab. He recently edited a book looking at changes and challenges in the world which will impact on business. A brief summary of this work is included in Figure 5.3.

Second, looking at the business model which shows how different aspects of business are brought together in a unifying way, the importance of the environment has again been highlighted. Here, we can see that a clear understanding of wider issues is a helpful starting-point to building a credible business strategy which is of primary importance in building up value for the owners of the business. There is a systematic approach to looking outward to discern those trends that will

Observations

1. Coping with the disintegration of value systems.
2. Maintaining global security.
3. The new inequalities.
4. Ensuring sustainability in an over-populated world.
5. Living in the new information society.
6. Keeping pace with a globalising economy.
7. Integrating Asia.
8. Creating sufficient employment.
9. Ensuring national policy-making in a global world.
10. Re-engineering the corporation.

Revolutions

1. Scope and use of information (positive).
2. The spread of the market economy (positive).
3. Reduced role of values in society (negative).
4. Reduced input of labour in production (negative).

Megatrends

1. The decreasing social and ecological sustainability of human existence.
2. The compression of time frames, the acceleration of change.
3. Increasingly complex agenda of international issues including:
   (a) the three of historical significance:
      - multilateral trade and monetary relations.
      - East–West military balance.
      - North–South global resource transfer.
   (b) Newer, emerging issues:
      - population explosion and challenges of urbanisation, ecology, sustainability, health care.
      - world crime, terrorism, drug trafficking.
      - nuclear proliferation.
      - migration.

Leadership requirements

- Vision of power must accommodate fragmentation of society.
- Power no longer derives from status.
- Leaders must recognise power of information and craft this into knowledge.
- Leaders must accept the reality of the market economy.
- Recognise that although labour is devalued, human beings should not be.

SOURCE: Derived by adapting conclusions from Klaus Schwab (ed.), *Overcoming Indifference*, 1995.

Figure 5.3 Schwab's observations

most impact on the business. We need to be able to pick up on the trends that will have greatest impact, the 'megatrends'. This is a topic to which we will return a little later in the chapter.

Rapid change

There is no doubt that because all managers operate in a world of rapid change, it will be clear that the operating environment in which they work is not constant. So far, in this chapter, we have looked at the environment as a part of the business model within the context of strategic planning. Another approach is to review the business literature to find common themes. As you would expect, this approach reinforces some of the observations already made. The key themes can be summarised under six headings:

1. *Technology* Each company will need to have a broad sweep of trends in technology and to understand the implications that will apply in the future to the industry or the company. The most spectacular example is the growing pervasiveness of information technology and its influence on all industries and firms.
2. *More global* Globalisation of business is increasing. Consumers are becoming more aware of world trends or fashions through satellite or cable television and are being influenced rapidly towards change. Dress habits, in India or China as examples, are becoming increasingly westernised and more and more people are travelling internationally. Within this theme, there are very strong regional blocks which will have a significant influence on business: the EU with its enlarged markets but unique rules, the NAFTA which has included low-cost areas of production and a large market, and ASEAN countries that may well form a more formidable block than present. All this adds a dimension, a complexity, that needs to be dealt with.
3. *Demographic issues* These will change according to country and region. The Western world will need to deal with an ageing population and the relatively lower number of people available to meet the demand for skilled labour. Other countries, like Indonesia or India, will continue to have a relatively young population while Ireland, also with its young population, may continue to see a migration of skilled top talent to bigger markets. The implications for social policy, for employment and for business are quite deep.

4. *Deregulation and regulation* It is a paradox that we have a freer world with less regulation in so many areas yet in others, substantial regulation. Regulatory changes can be rapid and the implications far-reaching as has been seen in the tobacco industry of the Western world, or as a different example in transportation.

5. *Aggregation and disaggregation* Mergers and takeovers will persist as parent companies continue the trend towards simplifying their businesses and selling off unwanted parts. On the other hand acquisitions will continue on a more global basis as companies position themselves more strongly within desired areas or form alliances on either a regional or worldwide basis.

6. *Values* Values, too, are changing and this will affect the organisation of the future. People will make more holistic choices about their lives, creating tension areas with firms. It will mean that employees will trade off opportunities and potential income for balance in their life or to take account of family aspirations and objectives. On the demand side, the pressure to provide variety will continue alongside the focus on value for money. Cheapness is not always synonymous with value in consumers' eyes and wise businesses are continually updating their knowledge base to ensure that they are aware of consumers' desires. Attention will need to be paid to the weighting of service, including a clear definition of what service is really required by customers.

In the next section of this chapter we will look briefly at an illustration of methodology that can be used to try to discover the big trends of greatest potential impact on the business. It is illustrative only, included here to demonstrate that it is possible to use a systematic approach to some of the difficult, softer issues to try to identify future opportunities or threats to the business which are posed by changes in the wide environment.

Megatrends

There are both business gurus and management consultants who focus on bringing together megatrends that will influence individual firms, the industries where they reside and even the economies in which they operate. Some of today's companies are trying to look systematically into the broad environment to provide insights that will influence their strategic choices. Some consulting firms have systematised this approach and will provide input to companies who are looking for a framework for conducting 'blue sky' strategy development. They identify key long-term trends which are likely to affect future demand. As an example, the LEK Partnership has an approach it has used with success in helping companies to develop corporate strategies or to 'pick winners' among a diverse range of investments.

This approach to megatrend analysis starts with getting an understanding of the different socio-economic trends in a particular geographic market or customer segment. For a geographic market, these might include the areas shown in Figure 5.4.

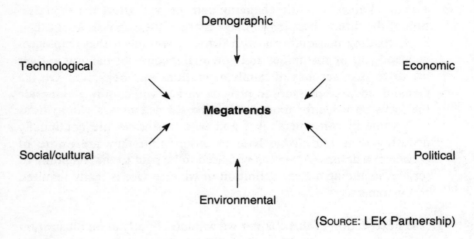

(SOURCE: LEK Partnership)

Figure 5.4   Finding megatrends

The initial analysis involves collecting together as much relevant information as possible on each of these areas based on government statistics, reports from special interest groups, market research surveys and books and articles by experts or by specialist forecasters. This research can then be synthesised to draw out what appear to be the 'megatrends' in each area. To illustrate this, Figure 5.5 shows some hypothetical responses that might be derived from the work.

This analysis is then applied to a particular market sector and used as the basis for identifying likely future customer behaviour and what products and services might meet those needs. The best forum for this may be one or more brainstorming sessions involving senior managers and outsiders. This is also an opportunity to bring in the wide experience of the non-executive directors who will enjoy such a session and usually

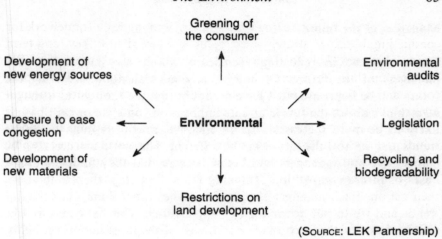

(SOURCE: LEK Partnership)

Figure 5.5 Identifying the impact of megatrends

add great value. The result of the brainstorming sessions will be a list of ideas for products and services which might be successful in the future. This can be used in a number of ways. For example, a company may use it as a basis for selecting which businesses within its portfolio have long-term development potential, identifying a future basis for competitive advantage and identifying what skills it needs to develop in order to be successful.

Implications for business

The importance of addressing the environment and seeing significant change implications for the company is not just a personal view. It is one that is shared both by industrial leaders and management writers like Prahalad and Hamel. In their book, *Competing for the Future*, they observe: 'We are standing on the verge and for some it will be the precipice of a revolution as profound as that which gave birth to modern industry. It will be the environmental revolution, the genetic revolution, the materials revolution, the digital revolution and, most of all, the information revolution.' They go on to develop the themes and to demonstrate that entirely new industries will be born, mega opportunities for new products and services will arise and they will mostly be global. Speed of action is encouraged to address these trends because of the time lag.

Managers of the future

There is value in reflecting specifically about the implications for managers of the future. Of course, any generalisation involving the future will be imprecise but I have no doubt that the thoughtful manager who thinks about the future and its implications on style or skill base is likely to be more successful. To be effective, managers must recognise trends and see how the future will be different. The world will certainly be competitive and managers had better be sure that they understand the bases of future competition. Thinking is the first step, then evaluation, then action. Each manager should, in a quiet time, think about major trends and try to put down a list of implications. This list could well be refined down further to provide a synthesis of the most important items. To stimulate the reader, Figure 5.6 lists some of the important implications.

Trends

- Speed of change is increasing
- More global
- Growing importance of emerging economies
- Fundamental role of information
- Rapid change in technology
- Greater demand for individuality both by workforce and customers
- Shorter life-cycles of products and technology
- Service is increasingly a source of differentiation
- Great complexity
- Important demographical changes will impact differently
- Mergers, acquisitions and disposals will increase

Implications for managers

- Need for strategic understanding, judgement and speed of action
- Need to cope with complexity
- International outlook essential
- Should be able to deal with diversity
- Need to be comfortable with change
- Should be widely aware, curious, forward-thinking
- Value broad experience
- Communication is key

Figure 5.6 Trends and implications

The process is considerably enriched when small teams get together to think systematically through company issues and implications for managers. They will pick the key trends that will have the greatest impact within the time frame selected and which have more specific implications for managers. Then, from this commonly agreed background, experienced managers will set down for themselves a personal action list which will better prepare them to be successful in the new order of things.

Summary

This chapter has looked broadly and generally at the environment with all that this applies. Some people will be discomfited by the lack of precision that inevitably flows from the scope included here. Others will find the very notion of thinking about these issues as crystal-ball-gazing which is not a reliable foundation for future actions. Despite the difficulties, I hold the view that there is value in systematically trying to think widely and about how trends might impact in the future.

We started out by noting that managers need to think broadly and look outwards more than is currently done today. The suggestion was made that this is important for managers who must not be continually swamped by the urgent. Next, the environment and changes within it were seen as an important first stage in the business model that helps to describe the processes by which business operates, finding systematic ways by which we can find and use trends that impact on the individual firm. Finally, we have looked at the implications both for business and for successful managers.

In all this there is no unique winning formula or secret to success. The best solution is the one most appropriate to the unique circumstances of the reader which must be individually worked through. The major benefit of this chapter will be to provide a framework to thinking and a stimulus to spend more time looking outward, thinking about the environment and the possible impact on the firm and its managers.

6   Strategy

A building block

Strategy is an essential building block for the company that is striving to maximise long-term value. It is based on the concept of finding a direction that yields a sustainable competitive advantage. To achieve this there is a need to analyse the wider environment, to pick out trends, to look carefully at customer requirements and to know in depth the qualities of competition. After the analysis and the evaluation, a strategy is defined which is a well-coordinated set of action programmes across the business, focused on longer-term value. To arrive at this position, the company will ensure linkage to the mission statement and be satisfied that the strategic plan builds from strengths to develop opportunities, but at the same time properly deals with the corporate weaknesses or threats to the business.

A well-thought-through strategy based on appropriate analysis, translated in action steps is for me a precursor to maximising shareholder value. The plan should be seen as a guide rather than a rigid route map. Inevitably, events will not turn out to be as predicted so that during the journey adjustments will need to be made. The contention is that to have a plan or a sense of direction is preferable to being without, for we can see when we are blown off course and understand the best way to respond.

There is a body of opinion that suggests that detailed planning is a fruitless exercise as energy is expended planning for events that do not occur as predicted. They also go further, giving examples where plans have been shattered because of an unpredicted significant event. An example might well be the oil crisis which sent shock waves through industry because it was totally unexpected and destroyed the careful scenario planning of a number of large companies.

There are also those detractors of strategy who would argue that in a world of rapid change the corporation is better to put its efforts into developing reactive speed, having an organisation perhaps of entrepreneurs that can take advantage of change. This thought is more completely argued in chaos theory which has a small body of converts who argue that planning is of little value given the chaos that abounds from the rapidly changing world.

86

I take a very different view. In my experience, a well-thought-through strategy provides value for the company in the following ways:

1. The quality of action plans will be improved given the deep thinking, the research and evaluation that takes place.
2. The attainable goal may well be higher as a result of this work.
3. You can be certain that all involved will know a great deal more about the broad environment, about customers, competition and alternative ways of winning.
4. There is a shared sense of direction which becomes the rallying cry for its people, building a cohesion of effort.

Admittedly, the environmental changes or unexpected competitive activity will cause variations or adjustments during the currency of the plan. I like the analogy of white-water rafting where each turn of the river brings the unexpected. The rafters will need to make navigational adjustments, perhaps even on occasions need to leave the river and go overland to avoid especially dangerous parts. This is better than aimlessly setting off without a plan or a goal.

Intuitive strategies

There are many examples of companies that have materially improved total value for shareholders through well-thought-through and well-executed strategy. Both aspects – that is the strategic thinking as well as the execution – are important. Endless case studies and published works support this view. However, there are also some companies that have almost fortuitously stumbled onto a winning strategy without the detailed analytical work envisaged here.

Such a company is Dynacast, a worldwide leading precision engineering company that specialises in small-size diecasting in zinc, aluminium, magnesium and engineering plastics. Dynacast started off as a diecaster of zip fasteners which require a reasonably high degree of precision in production if the zip is to be perfectly usable. It was soon discovered that Dynacast had special expertise that could be applied to other areas by using their high level of skills in tool-making and in making specialist machines so they diversified into other areas. The company grew from within itself, having an ability to innovate by seeing a wider array of new opportunities for their small, complex parts that would often save their customer a great deal of time in product assembly by using Dynacast subcomponents. Gradually, this company has grown to be worldwide with plants optimally placed to serve customers in the motor vehicle industry, in computers, radios, cellular telephones, DIY tools and promotional products. The people who developed this business were largely tool-makers who were promoted to general managers of small plants where they developed their commercial capabilities as well as core competences in the business. These core competences include the making of complex moulds, the ability to produce proprietary machines that give higher quality and lower costs than competitors and to develop the service culture which is so important.

Almost intuitively, they evolved an excellent strategy which is hard for the fragmented industry to follow and which is genuinely based on core capabilities. The only occasion that Dynacast went outside its niche into larger, almost commodity products, they were not successful and later sold off both a medical products and a pots and pans business. Today, this company is very profitable, has a turnover of £350 m, continues to grow at between 7 per cent and 10 per cent per annum, but does now fully utilise a planning process which they believe is very valuable. The conclusion is that even when a sound strategy evolves fortuitously, or perhaps intuitively, there is equally a possibility that it may also accidentally suboptimise its future. Value is created by using the disciplines which surround a good planning process.

The big idea

Strategy is not just about making minor adjustments to the current direction to respond to changes in competitor actions or customer needs. Strategic thinking should be focused on the big idea that will make a difference and which is then evaluated for both risk and reward as well as for feasibility of implementation. Typically, these big ideas evolve from more lateral thinking processes where those concerned 'think the unthinkable' as they try to bridge the gap between the company's current position and where it would like to be in the future.

There are some general observations about strategy which are worth consideration:

1. Strategy is competitive, requiring careful, thoughtful analysis of markets, and competition through an understanding of the strengths, weaknesses, opportunities and threats (SWOT analysis). It also follows that the strategy will address the competitive battlefield choosing an area of strength rather than playing to competition rules.

'What business are we in?' is often the question asked here and, perhaps more importantly, 'which one should we be in?'

2. Strategy process requires managers to review the broader environment to pick up trends, implications for the future and how these will impact on the corporation. This will indicate industry attractiveness, new product areas, threats or opportunities that need to be addressed.

3. The unifying features of the strategy should provide a coherent set of actions that galvanise the organisation together bound by a common purpose. In other words, the strategy becomes the framework in which the firm is able to set personal objectives across the organisation.

The process

Textbooks abound with detailed approaches to the process of strategy. Perhaps the best-known author is Michael Porter, who has helped business people to focus on the competitive nature of strategy. This has drawn attention to the need to analyse an industry fully for its relative attractiveness and to understand clearly the role of competitors, taking into account their reactions when strategic moves are made. In 1985, Porter first published his work *Competitive Advantage: Creating and Sustaining Superior Performance*. This book followed on from his earlier work, *Competitive Strategy*, and both are important references for managers today. His work is a constant reminder of the need for appropriate analysis of the key factors that impact on competitiveness in the industry where the firm participates. Porter's now-famous diagram is a model of clarity of factors that influence industry attractiveness and implications of competition on a company's strategy. The simplified version of Porter's diagram of competitiveness is set out in Figure 6.1.

The second area of strategic thinking to which I would like to refer is best encapsulated in Gary Hamel and C. K. Prahalad's work, *Competing for the Future*. This book, first published in 1994, observed that many business strategies deal with relative competitive advantage but they fail to capture the dynamic of competence-building. They also noted that in their considerable experience this notion of having a core competence perspective is not a natural one to most companies or businessmen they have observed. Yet it is fundamental if a company is to be attractive in the future. Perhaps the most important point of all to underline is that the businessman cannot rest until he has seen how the identified core

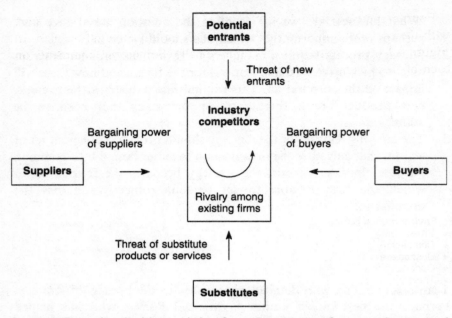

SOURCE: Reproduced with permission from *Competitive Advantage: Creating and Sustaining Superior Performance*, The Free Press, 1985, p. 5, with permission of Michael Porter and Harvard Business School Press.

Figure 6.1 Porter's five competitive forces that determine industry profitability

competences can be translated into action steps that will deliver sustainable competitive advantage over time.

This focus is now being embedded into the strategic plans of forward-thinking companies that are determined to build more robust strategies in a changing world. Quality analysis is needed to see new opportunities that can be within the grasp of any business and an objective detailed measure of core competences as needed. There are examples of companies that have developed new competences (just as there are some that have become obsolete) but this does take time and real effort.

Management consultants also have their own approaches to strategic planning which they are eager to share. In this section we will look at the key elements of the process rather than provide a detailed treatise on strategic planning. For those wanting a more detailed approach there are plenty of good books. A comprehensive book which covers in rigorous fashion the key elements in a thorough, structured way, written by Hax and Majluf and entitled *The Strategy Concept and Process: A Practical Approach*, will provide excellent reference material.

For me, there are seven key elements of the strategy process which start with the corporate mission and end up with an implementation plan. In Figure 6.2 these are set out diagrammatically. Some brief comments on each of these elements follow:

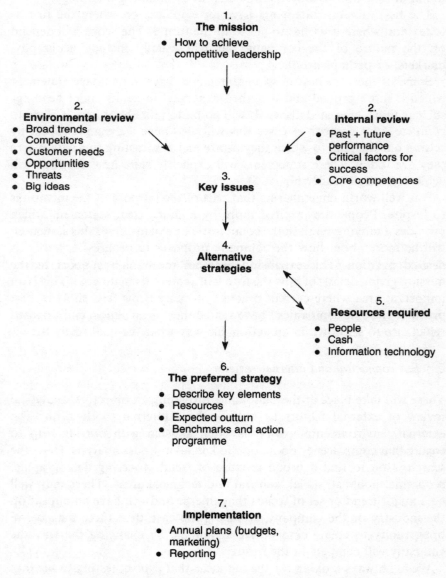

1.
The mission
- How to achieve competitive leadership

2.
Environmental review
- Broad trends
- Competitors
- Customer needs
- Opportunities
- Threats
- Big ideas

2.
Internal review
- Past + future performance
- Critical factors for success
- Core competences

3.
Key issues

4.
Alternative strategies

5.
Resources required
- People
- Cash
- Information technology

6.
The preferred strategy
- Describe key elements
- Resources
- Expected outturn
- Benchmarks and action programme

7.
Implementation
- Annual plans (budgets, marketing)
- Reporting

Figure 6.2 Seven elements of the strategy process

1. Mission

The mission sets out the broad expression of the purpose of the business with an uplifting or motivational statement explaining how it expects to achieve the excellence or competitive advantage required. It is aspirational in tone and usually the first step in formulating a strategy.

The best mission statements have an emphasis on where the firm is today and where it wishes to get to in the future. The scope will depend on the nature of the company but will usually include geography, markets, or perhaps products.

Some of the very best mission statements have a summary statement which is more general and it is then expanded in detail under headings such as those suggested above. It will go on to talk about how it plans to compete. In a number of cases this will also have a dynamic aspect by setting out the goal to which they aspire and contrasting this with where they are today. These statements will explicitly state how the firm will achieve strategic leadership.

It is well worth remembering that part of the purpose of the mission is to inspire. People are inspired more by a short, clear statement which provides a rallying-point in the company. The expansion of this statement will be more about how the company proposes to progress towards its desired position. This expansion becomes more of a support to the mission giving details of how the firm will achieve its main goal. This is an important area where current practice of many firms falls short of best practice. In some companies I have visited there is an almost embarrassed reluctance to set down in an actionable way what the goal really is.

2. Environmental and internal reviews

These will take place at the same time, providing an objective, analytical review of external factors as well as those internal to the firm. The external, environmental review is often assisted with outside help to ensure that complacency does not blind an all in-house analysis. Here, the search is on to find a broad mixture of trends covering demographic, economic, political, social, cultural and technical areas. There may well be a major trend or set of trends that emerge and will have an impact on the industry or the company. If this is the case then there may be an opportunity to create competitive advantage by changing the way the company will compete in the future.

We are always looking for the big ideas that evolve, testing to see that these are compatible with the areas of core competence residing in the

Corporation. Random but interesting big ideas that do not fit the company's present or future strategic direction must be left. Focus must be maintained.

With the internal review, navel-gazing is the key activity. It is an objective, inward look to see if the armoury of abilities matches up to the requirements of the strategy. Where the strategy has been in place for a time, the questions the managers will be asking are: 'Is the strategy working, delivering the expected performance?'; 'If not, what changes are needed to meet legitimate goals?'

When both the internal and environmental review have been completed, the business will have the well-recognised list of strengths, weaknesses, opportunities and threats (or SWOT analysis). This is a helpful list only if it goes beyond the superficial. If there are strengths there is the obligation to understand how to exploit these for competitive advantage. Remember, the SWOT analysis must provide real insights and must be in sufficient detail to enable actions to be taken.

3. Key issues

This is the distillation stage where there is an action list that will need to be fully addressed in the various strategies available. They will be the big issues that will influence strategy or any amendment to existing strategy. The list will vary by business but might include the unexpected entrance of a new competitor, market factors such as changes in GATT, new alliances in the industry, changes in supply to the business or the impact of new technology.

4. Alternative strategies

There is always strategic choice and never only one alternative. However, if an agreed strategy is in place, is working and broadly delivering the benefits then this step can be skipped. Where the firm judges that a review of alternatives is necessary, they will need to allow some extra time for the iterative loop that would be programmed into the process. It is also true that different strategies will have different claims on resource which will need to be fully evaluated. Some corporations require that the alternative strategies also be evaluated financially using net present value calculations. This follows because if a board is to commit to one of the alternatives it needs to understand in financial terms the choice it is making. This is a helpful, disciplined way to view the choices but it would be wrong to assume that at this stage the numbers are other than broadly indicative as opposed to a financially perfected plan. The danger of this approach is that the planning process may become financially driven which would be a major mistake. The exercise is strategic with approximate numbers as a by-product. We need competitive understanding, creativity and good judgement in making the choice.

5. *Resources required*

People with the right skills, motivation and drive, in the numbers required will be needed to deliver the chosen strategy. Equally, the strategy chosen must be manageable within the culture of the corporation. It may well be that strategy shifts are being used to change a culture that is more empathetic to the forward environment. However, where significant changes are needed time must be allowed for this. Usually, this will take longer than expected! An objective appraisal of the people requirement of the plan is key. In many cases the speed of implementation may well be constrained by the need to build up the people resource. When the plan is described, then the necessary training, recruitment or redeployment must be arranged for the people who are to carry it out or, if necessary, a company that already has the skills in place, must be acquired.

Cash constraints need to be recognised as the board of directors will certainly wish to address the funding plan and to understand any balance-sheet risk implicit in this. I have also separated out information technology as often this is a competitive differentiator or a constraint to the implementation of a strategy. Certainly, where strategy calls for acquisition of a company to be integrated this requires very specific attention and the speed of implementation may well be affected by the systems requirements. In any event, the information technology and information plan must be compatible with the strategy and fully capable of supporting the major initiatives described in it.

6. *The preferred strategy*

This is the working document that will guide the executives in their execution. The key elements are:

- A description of the key elements of the plan.
- Details of the resources required to deliver the plan and how these will be provided.
- The expected outturn of the plan in objective, measurable terms. This would include the financial outturn using key headline numbers for sales, operating profits, operational cash flow, capital spend and

special development spend together with broad balance-sheet implications. Other items such as market share, new market penetration or new technologies would also be included.

- The key strategic benchmarks with dates and finite measures so that management can check at critical staging posts that the strategy is working. It is also useful to have an action programme at this time with allocation, responsibilities and timings clearly identified.

7. Implementation

Although this occurs last in the sequence it is of most critical importance. Without good implementation even the best strategy is close to useless. Strategy is not a free-standing, isolated process. It is integrated within the management processes of a corporation. Therefore, the budget of year 1 of the business plan will be linked to strategic planning. The detailed budget will need to broadly match expectations from the plan both as to financial progress and claims for resource. The strategy being followed in the budget will of course agree with the plan although adjustments may well be needed due to elapsed time.

Once the budgets are agreed through the normal detailed evaluation process, through challenging and negotiation, they become the basis upon which the business is measured. Typically, a marketing plan will be prepared at this time to support the budget and this, too, will set out details behind the budget assumptions. All this provides the basis for controlling the company against agreed parameters using an information system that is helpful and time-saving, dwelling on exceptions yet giving access as required to detail.

Communication of strategy

Especially where businesses devolve decision-making as close as possible to the point of impact, there is a need to ensure the communication of a consistent, strategic message throughout the organisation as well as to outside stakeholders. The message will need to be pitched at the different target audiences within an overall framework. Coherence is necessary if strategy is to be a unifying force within the company and understood outside. The 'no surprises' rule is important for each of the audiences who should feel comforted by the common understanding that decisions taken by the management are compatible with or supportive of the stated position.

─── **Case Study 6.1** ───

Confused strategy

London International Group is a company registered on the London Stock Market with a market capitalisation of around £300m. It is best-known for its leadership in condoms and, using the same technology, produces household gloves and medical gloves. It has held world leadership in condoms over the past 10 years and has market presence around the world. This has always been the core business of the company.

The company's past performance has been shaky and its strategy confused. In the 1980s, when the company was led by a dominant chairman–chief-executive, it built a broad health and beauty division of peripheral proprietary products in which other major healthcare companies were not interested. Products like gripe water, cough elixirs, manicure sets and toothpaste for heavy smokers were grouped together to form a second division. The company diversified still further and entered the chinaware market to which it tried to add a further acquisition that it was unable to complete. This division was subsequently sold as a result of a re-evaluation of strategy. However, LIG was soon to enter another totally unrelated field in photo-processing. Predictably enough, it did this by acquisition and topped up the primary acquisition with a number of infill acquisitions both in the United Kingdom and Europe.

Looking back, the company had a leadership position in condoms and core competence in moulding thin fabrics of latex. Their new 'Biogel' powderless surgeon's glove was a genuine innovation that grew from the capabilities of the company which were competitively sustainable. However, as the largest market for this new product was in the USA, a significant resource investment was needed to get regulatory approval. Given the size of the opportunity and the resources of LIG, this should have been their first priority.

The Health and Beauty Division was, in reality, made up of a ragbag of brands that were of little value individually. Although at first sight the channels of distribution were compatible with condoms, there was very little synergy in practice. At best, this division was always going to be buffeted by the major pharmaceutical companies and to compete with Proctor & Gamble or Unilever was a very uneven competition! In the late 1980s and early 1990s new acquisitions were again widely scattered and geographically different, but the division was stretched across countries with very few areas of geographical strength.

The Photo-processing Division was never a financial success. It was free-standing, a difficult 'people' business to manage and one where margins were being squeezed quite badly due to intensified competition. The total market was badly affected by both the European recession and a poor summer in 1993 which both meant that fewer photographs were taken. LIG closed the loss-making Spanish operation and finally, in 1994, withdrew from all photo-processing, selling this division to its management for a nominal sum.

These excursions into unrelated business destroyed significant shareholder value. The company had a rights issue in 1990 to reduce the gearing which was around 100 per cent but then frittered that cash away on numerous small acquisitions in peripheral areas. In 1994, a further rights issue was made to rescue the company from insolvency.

LIG is now under new management led by Nick Hodges as Chief Executive, focused on the core activities of condoms and gloves. To give an idea of the destruction of value caused over the previous years:

		£m
	Market capitalisation 31 December 1990	345
plus	Rights issue January 1991	62
plus	Rights issue June 1994	115
	Total value (historic)	522
	Approximate market cap 1995	300
	Shareholder value destroyed	222

Key Lessons

1. Strategy was inadequate. A rationale for the diversifying moves was constructed at the time but was not based on competitive advantage or core competences of the group.
2. Insufficient top-level debate of strategy coupled with a powerful chairman–chief-executive did not provide the required checks and balances.

There are five levels of communication each of which will have a common core of strategy but each requires a different level of detail or style of communication. Peeling back each layer at a time, we start with the external, and move to the internal levels.

1. *External*

This will include all the outside stakeholders, starting with shareholders, especially the institutions that are the company's biggest shareholders. Analysts who follow the company will need to have a clear understanding of the mission, the key building blocks in its execution which will be updated each year. Typically, a company will meet formally with analysts as well as key shareholders at least annually when they can talk through aspects of strategy. This provides a setting of mutuality so that management actions are credible. There are of course important other external stakeholders to consider. The core message on strategy will remain the same but it is possible that when communicating with major customers much more detail will be provided in the areas of major mutual interface. Customers need to understand the central thrust, be assured of the company's capability to serve them now and into the future. The tricky area which needs to be managed arises when, in executing the strategy, the corporation plans to sell off part of the business that may well have implications for the customer. This is a message best left until the event is near instead of announcing intentions well in advance. In the circumstance of a disposal the customers' concerns for continuity need to be fully taken to account.

The position with suppliers is not too dissimilar. If a partnership supplier understands his customer's strategy and long-term goals there is every chance he will reflect this in his own forward plans. Investment can be made that will help the supplier's customers and reinforce the bond between them.

We will see in Chapter 8 that the way we communicate is key to the message being received clearly. The annual report is often used as the first line of communication conveying a general sense of direction and also an objective review of past performance in relation to the strategy.

2. *At board level*

The board will have participated throughout the process, agreeing the broad mission and the key planks of the strategy. To that extent, the board is a partner in the strategy of the firm and there should be no surprises. Many boards will, during the strategy process, allocate special time to review the strategy against the broad environmental setting. Typically, a day will be reserved for this event but longer will be required if the company is complex or changing strategies. This will be followed by the business strategy being agreed by the board after it has been formally presented in reasonable detail. The communication will typically cover the following headings:

- The environment, how it is changing and the implications for the firm.
- Understanding core competences of the firm.
- Key elements of the existing strategy and how it is delivering.
- New opportunities.
- Proposed adjustments to strategy.
- Resources required.
- Key benchmarks.

When the strategy is agreed, it becomes the backcloth of the board against which decisions are taken and resources are allocated. Involvement of the board is key if they are to make effective decisions during the year. However, the chief executive must take the responsibility with his management team for the creation of strategy and of course for its implementation. Strategy is the creature of the business leader, not of the board, and not of the corporate strategy staff person. The board is there to provide insights, balance, comment and tempering of proposals if required. It is not effective or indeed possible for a board of directors to be the creators of the strategy. The role of the specialist corporate strategy manager, is to be the facilitator, the exponent of best practice, the one who provides information and insights to help the general manager prepare a well-thought-through strategy. The key message with the board is communication through participation.

3. Top management

In many companies there will be two levels of top management. The first level consists of the chief executive and a small corporate team, while the second level comprises those running individual businesses organised on either a product group or geographical basis. Responsibility for the creation of the corporate strategy resides with the chief executive even though during the process his top team will be fully involved at key stages. The management board is often the place where these deliberations take place and certainly sufficient time must be allocated to do justice to this important aspect of management. Especially when a major change is taking place, the chief executive may well have brought in an outside consultant to bring rigour to the analysis and to bring fresh insights. The consultant will play a very important role in preparing the management for change and in ensuring that their views are fully understood in the organisation. He can also provide an external legitimacy that will speed up the process which is very important when a new general manager is in place and wants to use the first hundred days to make a strategic impact.

Those in the top team who are fully responsible for profits for sections of the corporation will need to have a clear understanding of the agreed corporate strategy and the implications of this on their own. They will be responsible within this framework for creating, articulating and implementing their own strategy. The wise group chief executive will ensure that he has early input into the divisional strategy and that he is appraised of key steps along the pathway. When the divisional strategy is complete it will typically be presented to a small, central team who will probe at underlying assumptions, the steps of progress and the final goal. When the strategy is agreed it becomes part of the overall corporate strategy presentation to the board.

There is a dual communication role here for the divisional general manager. He or she needs to communicate upwards, securing endorsement on key stages, and downwards to the middle management and workforce within the divisional domain. Almost invariably there will be an additional role of communicating with external stakeholders.

4. Middle management

Middle managers need to comprehend the key elements of group strategy and to understand the detail of their own particular business unit. Their involvement in the creation of strategy is likely to be more distant and therefore senior management responsible for their area need to be clear in sufficient detail to help middle managers do their job. Individual managers' objectives and personal goals will be tied back to the execution of strategy. Given that corporations today are striving to force decision-taking down as close as possible to the point of impact, strategic understanding is important as an influence to the quality of decision-making.

Middle managers are responsible for workforce briefings and they will be quickly exposed if they do not understand the strategy in sufficient detail to deal with the increasingly informed workforce questions. This group of middle managers is an important cog in the communication process. They will need help to pass on information using prepared material if they are expected to do a good job.

5. *Workforce*

Managers continue to underestimate the intelligence and latent ability of the workforce to contribute to strategy execution. This inevitably limits the success in implementation. Those who argue against communicating strategy will talk of potential problems with unions, especially if they work out that factory closures, for example, may follow from the strategy. Some see the workforce as antagonistic and unhelpful, concluding that it is best not to involve them in strategy or company performance. If this is the case, then it is the responsibility of management to create a more productive environment. One of the ways of achieving this is to tell people what is happening.

If we wish to inspire the workforce to higher standards of, say, service and quality, they are likely to be motivated to achieve this if they better understand the long-term strategic reasons for this. Should there be a gap in value provided by the company compared with that provided by its competitors then this understanding will help to win compliance for inevitable cost reductions. This is especially true when the costs incurred do not really add value to the final consumer or customer. There are also lots of examples where workforce participation has enabled 'blindingly obvious' decisions to be taken to provide a higher level of competitiveness. The workforce remains a significant source of untapped value which only a few companies are fully utilising.

Addressing problems with planning

To recap some of the real benefits of effective strategic planning:

- It creates new insights that will lead to greater competitive advantage.
- Learning is enhanced through a greater awareness of the operating environment, customer needs, competition and areas of risk or opportunity.
- Segmentation techniques give insights that will lead to management decisions that are not immediately obvious.
- It creates awareness of the long-term competitiveness of the firm which acts as a balance to the inevitable pressure for short-run benefits.

- It develops new skills in managers – creativity, innovation but also disciplined thinking.
- It acts as an important integrating link through the business to give a unification of purpose that would be difficult to imagine without the planning process.
- It is team-building and can be fun!

With all these potential benefits, why is it that some managers have had problems with strategic planning resulting in some cases with abandonment of the process? The first reason relates to the process itself. If the top management are not enthusiastic then the process is moribund and nothing more than an exercise in futility. There is no alternative to the chief executive owning the process and being the driver of it. Of course, he will get help from the corporate planning manager and his colleagues in his top team. Time must be allocated to this most important top management task. As we have seen from the survey described in the opening chapter, senior managers seldom spend enough time strategising.

The second area of potential turn-off may be found in the process itself. There are many planning systems that are too bureaucratic, full of forms and systems, relying on intricate computer models to churn out the desired outturn. Usually, these are coupled with a strong central strategic planning staff, committed to making an impact on the business. The truth is that the capable general manager does not need a strategic planner at all, although most will find it helpful to have a limited resource of high calibre to help with staff work and perhaps as a stimulant to new thinking. The process should not be mechanical and should enable good, creative thinking to shine through.

The third area is where the planning process is free-standing and not interlinked with other processes. I prefer a simple, common database which can be used to cross-reference to the budget numbers. The strategic plan must, as we have seen, be linked with the 'people plan' together with understanding organisation consequences, the information technology plan and the marketing plan. It needs to be part of the fabric of the total business.

Observations

The process of strategy is a logical one that leads to change. Shareholders, the owners of the business, are entitled to expect that the strategy selected will, in the long term, deliver superior returns based on achieving a sustainable competitive advantage. The strategy will look at the different arenas in which it can compete, choosing that which is the most attractive and which is likely to match the current or planned future competences of the business. Managers must decide how best they can win in the chosen arena. Will it be through access to the market which others may find more difficulty to enter? This is not always a safe source of long-term advantage as we have seen with the airline industry for example when deregulation was 'discovered'. It may be through control of a proprietary asset such as a trademark or product licence, but again, complacency needs to be avoided if the company is not to be outflanked. More importantly, it may well be based on competences that differentiate the company from its competitors – cost, quality, service and flexibility are all relevant examples.

There are further choices to be made on how to improve the position in particular markets. The firm needs to decide which markets are the best, how it can change those markets for advantage and how many markets they can participate in. The question of focus is a very real one for there are many examples of firms seduced into complexity with all the attendant costs of this because of their lack of focus.

The manager needs to understand the potential performance, be clear about today's position and see the gap as the area to which he can add unique value as he energises the organisation to achieve the benefits within an acceptable time frame. Strategy is essential. It need not be complex or require rocket science to create. There is no doubt that the best strategies are well-thought-through, competitively focused and have a few concrete steps that will make a major difference to long-term performance. The advice is to keep it simple.

7 Adding Value

The core of all management activities is to add value. This must be the prime objective of all activities undertaken by managers. There are many different ways that value can be added and at every level of management the successful manager will understand the unique areas where most value can be created. Adding value is at the root of all management endeavours and is of course the core message of this book. Throughout this, ideas bubble around because a successful management team understands that collectively they must add so much value that their business is able to outperform the competition and provide superior financial returns in the long term. This message is present throughout, yet in this chapter we will examine six specific areas which experience has shown will yield significant benefits in the longer-term competitiveness of the firm:

1. Strategy;
2. Sales-based growth;
3. Fundamental review of the business processes to invest behind those that add value and scrap those that do not;
4. Information technology;
5. The value the group or the centre can add to a multidimensional business;
6. Can the board add value?

Inevitably, there is some overlap with other areas but that is normal in management. It is not usual to find knowledge or activities in prescribed little boxes!

Through strategy

Perhaps the greatest source of long-term added value is through strategic actions which, as we have seen in Chapter 6, will be derived from an objective process. Vital to success in this area is the ability to be proactive in a changing world and to seize new opportunities which will enable a company to take significant advantage over a more docile competition.

In a changing environment, successful companies will first have understood their real strategic capability and then used this to disrupt the competition. There is nothing terribly new about this approach, for indeed the entrepreneurs of old have practised this over many years. Economists too have recognised the role of innovation which can be used to disrupt the equilibrium thus yielding a margin for this legitimate activity. Sometimes this approach is referred to as 'thinking outside the box' emphasising a break from the status quo which is capable of being managed. It is important to remember that for creative thinking to be of practical benefit it needs to be contained within the bounds of properly identified core competences.

Adding value through the creative use of strategy is one of the most fruitful areas for consultants to generate business and also to add value. Sometimes the use of consultants can speed up the process and provide fresh insights that elude the 'home team' from the company. In these cases the best results are obtained by having a mixed team resourced from both the consultant and the company but with ownership at a responsible level within the company.

Whether managers choose to add value independently or to use consultants with the varied strategy products there are clearly identifiable steps that can be deduced. The approach is as follows:

1. Scan the broad environment to provide evidence of change that will affect the industry and the company.
2. Review and establish the core capabilities of the business differentiating these from the competition and understanding how these can be used competitively to derive value.
3. Look at the total chain of value alongside the suppliers and customers to see if there are mutual opportunities to integrate or remove business processes.
4. Creatively search for growth opportunities in new, perhaps unanticipated ways:
   - networking across geography;
   - related products, perhaps in adjacent areas.
5. Fundamental reviews to remove unprofitable complexity or to strip out the sins of averaging. Appropriate segmentation analysis will help provide these insights, just as activity-based management will provide a radically new way of looking at activities in the company.
6. Agree an action programme that focuses resource and activity on the areas of greatest potential. This will encapsulate the hard and soft issues to be managed as part of the change programme.

One of the best examples of adding value through strategy comes from Japan. Shima Seiki is a very successful company best known for the manufacture of industrial knitting machines for the clothing market. Through the remarkable insight of the President, Dr Masahiro Shima, the company has grown to dominate its core sector of knitting machines, having a market share of about 65 per cent in 28 years of history. It has done this through identifying trends from its environmental sweeps, developing the core capabilities to differentiate its product through providing service and solutions to customers' problems, so helping to make profit for them. They are now developing their core capability in information technology software and hardware to develop a completely new area which is already attracting worldwide attention. Case Study 7.1 sets out the detail.

Through sales-based growth

There is no doubt that sales growth adds considerable value, not only to the bottom line but crucially through giving confidence to the organisation. Most industries will find that given some operational leverage (the ability to extract marginal output from the same capacity and fixed costs), volume gains will deliver an incremental 20 to 30 per cent onto the bottom line. Needless to say, there are some real snags to consider.

Volume growth is seldom sustainable from price initiatives unless of course the company has a genuinely lower cost base. It is easily matched by competition. In the fashion industry, for example, key drivers of growth are design and innovation which are best delivered from a team of people committed to winning. It is not readily programmable to guarantee repetitive wins but there is a systemised approach that scans trends to make prediction easier and innovative responses more certain. Equally, speed of response in fashion is critical if the retailer is not going to face either, on the one hand, the extreme of running out of stock because of a low ability to replenish quickly, or on the other to be left with obsolete stock.

Within fast-moving consumer goods, volume gains may only be possible after a year or two of revenue investment which may raise the dilemma of timing, to trade-off short-run profits and cash flow, in the expectation of greater rewards further out. In the case of pharmaceuticals, the lead time is even longer given the more fundamental research requirements and the time required for the approval process.

———— Case Study 7.1 ————

Shima Seiki – value through strategy

Shima Seiki is based at Wakayama, near Osaka in Japan. Currently, it has sales in excess of US$500 million and is very profitable. It holds 65 per cent of the world's industrial-knitting-machine market which it has built up through organic growth over its 28 years of history. The powerhouse behind this growth is the company's President, Dr Masahiro Shima, who has been key to its success through the years. Initially, the company developed the capability of producing seamless, shaped, knitted gloves which are widely used in Japan. Shima Seiki soon dominated this market and was looking for growth opportunities. The knitting machines for fashion knitted garments were large, relatively high cost, difficult to change from one style to the next and required very skilled operators to link up the panels that had been knitted separately. The early 'non-fashion' knitting machines could not knit into shapes, so the knitted panels had to be cut, producing waste and requiring extra operations.

Dr Shima and his team recognised an opportunity based on their core competence of shaped, seamless knitting from their glove operations. They could save cost through reducing knitted fabric waste and by reducing the labour needed to make up the garment. The team also observed, from the environmental scan, that the fashion industry was one of rapid change where innovation and quick response was at a premium. They therefore designed garment knitting machines that could be rapidly changed over to any design through the use of electronics. Over the years, the system has been continuously improved so that today the machines can be linked with the computer-aided design (CAD) system to design the product on the screen, transform this into different colourways, produce technical knitting instructions for their production machine and transfer this automatically to commence knitting without a break in the process.

As a demonstration for me, they designed a ladies' jumper which I was able to alter, converted this to a set of technical knitting instructions to the knitting machines and have the actual garment available in two hours, packaged and ready to wear.

According to Dr Shima, the company has developed the following core competences which it has used to deliver competitive advantage:

- Software and hardware knowledge which is leading edge.
- Providing intensive total service to every customer: 'Shima provide total solutions not just machines.'

- Producing everything in-house to ensure that total service is maintained and that Shima are knowledgeable in every area.
- They have specialised in 'mechatronics' or the interface between mechanical engineering and electronics.
- Research and development is a priority to stay ahead of competition and to benefit from environmental trends (they have a staff of 200 R&D researchers out of a total staff of less than 1000).

'The guiding light at Shima Seiki is total service. We always think "customer in", whereas ten years ago we were focused on "product out"', says Dr Shima. Their dedication to service is very real. One of their major customers to whom I spoke told of an electronic random fault in two of their fifty new machines. The Shima response was to send more than 20 Japanese engineers to the United Kingdom to replace all the microchipboards during the Christmas shut-down.

The story does not finish here. Dr Shima is clear that the same principles can apply to communications and they are currently working on computer graphic design that will seriously reduce time and costs. In partnership with two other big Japanese companies, they can produce 'on-demand printing'. As an example, Shima are able to take camera input, produce colour separations and print instantly, and in small lots of say 6000 copies at relatively low costs. This means, for example, that they can see a fashion show in Paris, transmit visuals back to Japan by satellite and use a CAD system to put the designs or altered designs onto visuals of models held in their library. A brochure can be produced in 24 hours, compared with the more normal six to ten weeks of a traditional system.

The computer graphic design system evolved in the same way as their knitting-machine developments. Shima have leveraged their core competences across another avenue identified through their knowledge of relevant trends in the environment. They are now trying to use the computer design service in the print industry for graphics on television both in Japan and the USA, as well as in the clothing industry.

Today, their business remains vibrant and successful with sales as follows:

	% of total sales	% market share
Glove-making machine	10	90
Knitting machines for garments	70	65
Computer graphic design system	20	n/a

Gains through outstanding service are also the source of added value. This process starts with obtaining a really deep understanding of what the customer truly values and will pay for. Service is a key differentiator and often the source of premium pricing. In the uniforms supply business, customers like British Rail would traditionally put out the supply contract for quote. Because the business was large the potential supply companies, knowing that success would equate to low price, bid very keenly on a marginal cost basis. The industry was unprofitable.

Compton Sons & Webb, a leading supply company, broke the mould. They recognised that this approach was unprofitable to the supplier and quite high cost to the purchaser. British Rail had high stocks, a large administration resource and unhappy workers supplied with 'hit or miss'-fitting uniforms. Comptons proposed to British Rail that they would supply a specially sized pack to every employee, they would be responsible for stock and administration for a cost per person. Comptons were expert on quick-response fittings for even the most unusually sized employee, they would work on lower stocks and had developed a computer system that enabled them to provide the service. Margins were much improved and British Rail were happy on cost grounds as well as employee satisfaction. It will now be very difficult to dislodge Compton Sons & Webb provided they maintain this excellent service because they have 'brickwalled' the account, i.e. made entry difficult for a competitor.

Many companies all too readily accept that their products or services are approaching the end of a life cycle so that sales and profits will decline in the future. The phrase 'mature products' or a 'commodity business which is mature' can be heard amongst some managers who struggle with the dynamics of the marketplace. This is an unacceptable concept for I emphatically believe the old adage that 'there is no such thing as mature products, only mature managers'. Charles Baden-Fuller and John Stopford put it succinctly and upfront when they say, in *Rejuvenating the Mature Business*, that 'maturity is a state of mind'.

The creative management team will readily see that there are unique ways of creating value through innovation, altering the mix between product and service or addressing the cost base through business process re-engineering. The point is that the choice of territory upon which the firm will compete is management's. Equally the top team must be galvanised into action towards a common goal.

Provided that the management team is well-led and is committed to rejuvenation it is possible to deliver value to shareholders through well-thought-through, innovative, market-led strategies. Invariably the greatest focus is on the customer as the source of value while the delivery will depend, as always, on the excellence of the management team, their 'can do' attitude and their will to win.

Yet even with something as apparently uncontroversial as volume growth, there are conflicting tensions that need to be resolved. Incremental product groups, brands or stock-keeping units can only be added to the point where the additional profits are offset by the costs of complexity. This, in concept terms, is easy to grasp. However, often the firm's accounting system has no way of highlighting the costs of complexity in practice. Costs are usually captured under cost centres such as wages, salaries and rent. Therefore the manager who wishes to understand the real costs will need to dig deeper than the superficial numbers on the company's accounting system.

Searching out new customers or new products is often seen as a good thing *per se*. We know that innovation is to be applauded and often the fruits of innovative initiatives will be new products, new brands or new customers. This needs to be balanced with the costs of achieving and sustaining this new area, comparing the net benefits of the approach with the alternative. It is possible that the alternative of spending the new investment money on loyal, regular customers is more beneficial. There is now a growing body of opinion which emphasises that building quality and long-term transaction value in customer relationships often has a better payback. There is quality evidence that demonstrates that traditional businesses over-invest in soliciting new customers and neglect at their cost the opportunity of building long-term relationships with their customers. If companies are to understand their customers better they need to be properly segmented and an appropriate marketing database set up. Traditional analysis gives only base-level information which is difficult to act upon. A retailer operating effective databased marketing will want to know more about personal preferences, attitudes and aspirations if a rapport is to be built leading to true loyalty. The end result is not just to gain this valuable customer knowledge but also to act as a catalyst to the whole business to raise its sights, perform better by really understanding and serving the customer in every respect.

While there is potential value from sales-generating strategies which will be different for different companies, managers need to understand the implications very clearly. They will need to watch the cost side of this sales/growth equation to make sure that the long-term potential of the firm is enhanced.

Through re-engineering business process

Typically, companies of today are organised on principles of yesterday. Often they are over-layered with a bias to functions and have business processes that reflect history and fail to identify those processes which their customers most value.

Ask managers how they would like their organisation to be seen and the following word-picture emerges:

- competitive
- customer-focused
- efficient
- innovative
- de-layered
- lean
- nimble
- open
- responsive.

Check actuality against the word-picture and you will usually find a lack of congruence in a number of areas. Often the reason for this will be found in the fact that the total business chain of value from base supplier through to manufacturer, distributor and customer is not approached as a whole. Each segment looks in detail at its own area, trying to create value even at the expense of someone else in the chain and to capture that value for themselves.

Today, companies are looking in depth at the key things they do, to distinguish between those that really add value for customers and those that do not. Involvement of the customers in the process helps to bond the supplier to them, understanding more clearly their needs or desires. The key point to remember apart from this mutuality in the value chain is that processes that do not add value should be scrapped.

The process is not just a cost reduction exercise, even though large reductions in costs will surely be thrown up. Investments in real customer value-added areas are also likely so that there is a genuine strategic dimension. Strategy must be the first priority. To achieve this there is a re-aggregation of tasks to bring together a value-adding business process. This of course is in sharp contrast to the observation of Adam Smith who, in 1776, recognised that a division of labour improved productivity and quality in his example of pin-making.

Perhaps an example will make these points clearer. The clothing industry has a degree of riskiness attached to it by the nature of the fashion element as the fickle consumer does not always react in a predictable way. At the retail level it can be seen that you are in a no-win situation. If you over-buy inventories are too high and markdowns sky-rocket, having a major negative impact on profitability. If you under-buy you lose sales to the competition. In effect, the consumer is being asked to pay more because of the system's inability to forecast sales accurately. Usually these firms are organised in a traditional, functional way. While costs are important, the ability to anticipate and respond quickly are critical. A number of processes are duplicated between the supplier and the customer and a number of processes which do not add value can be identified including progressing raw materials, shifting raw material between different sites, changes between design and production to get optimal production, batch progressing, central warehousing, and delivery first to the customers' central warehouse then to their regional warehouse. Throughout all of this there are mistakes, frustration and a lack of accountability and cost which produces no value for the customer.

As another example, BHS, a leading retailer in the United Kingdom, has been moving aggressively with a few key suppliers to re-engineer their systems. They targeted significant uplifts in performance by benchmarking their performance with the best. The opportunity was great with a potential 25 per cent uplift in sales if all items demanded could be in stock while avoiding excessive mark-downs. This gave rise to a significant initiative called the 'Breakthrough Initiative' which looked at radical ways of improving performance through re-engineering processes, especially buying. They wanted to uplift financial performance through:

- improving product availability from 76 per cent to 92 per cent;
- reducing stock from 14 weeks to five or six;
- reducing lead times from between 70 to 190 days (depending on product) to closer to 50 days;
- utilising focused supplier relationships and appropriate computer aided design technology.

The BHS value-adding processes are to create the product, make the product and move the product with the minimum of time. By re-engineering the business process, the total cycle time for a simple garment will be between 10 and 40 days, dealing with just one or two responsible suppliers – an improvement on the the current position which takes between four and nine months, involving 13 buyers (all with a paper trail), 37 suppliers who will have 22 raw material suppliers each and too many warehouse stock movements!

The bottom-line potential for BHS is huge as they will benefit from:

- increased sales through greater availability;
- much lower mark-downs;
- improved margin through reduced costs of sampling, lower costs and economies of scale;
- much-reduced inventory through just-in-time deliveries (JIT) from suppliers;
- improved quality;
- reduced overheads internally and where duplicated with suppliers.

The number of suppliers has already been reduced from 750 to under 400 and the target is to reduce further towards 100. The process of developing value-managed relationships is a key element in the management of the supply chain.

It is an exciting development for BHS as they have aimed high, seen the move as strategic, involved key suppliers and, importantly, involved their customers.

The concept of re-engineering business process is important and cannot be ignored by any general manager. It is a major source of value, has strategic implications and requires real management time. Many managers do not understand the wide scope of its application to their every day business. They can limit it to encompass laying off people or merely as an information technology plaything. Many consultants have specialty areas of competence in this area and there are a number of easy-to-read books which will provide back-up material. Michael Hammer and James Champy have published an easy-to-read introduction called *Re-engineering the Corporation* which provides useful background with some detailed case studies.

Through information technology (IT)

First, in this age of change where speed is important, where information is essential, the role of IT is a key ingredient in delivering the strategy. In fact, there are many examples where IT has given a company a genuine competitive advantage. Two such examples are the American Airlines reservation system which gave advantage to American Airlines in bookings from travel agents, and Thomson Holidays who sell packaged holidays abroad and who introduced their TOP (Travel order processing) system into travel agents' offices.

Managers need to think widely about how IT can give advantage. At the Design Centre in Nottingham, a design service for the clothing interests of Coats Viyella Plc, extensive use is made of computer-aided design (CAD) with direct links with the major customer, Marks & Spencer. This enables a designer at Nottingham to interface with a product selector at M&S in London to change and agree a design instantly.

Using a special in-house software package, the design is printed from the screen directly onto cloth and a sample garment can be made up, packaged and be on the M&S selector's desk the next morning. Previously, designs were produced and changed once or twice before a sample was made up, taking from two to four weeks.

The same process can also be used where fabric printing is undertaken in-house by automatically transferring instructions from the screen to engrave the printing plates (there are often up to 25 colours) avoiding much cost, errors and six weeks work.

Looking for a moment to the role of electronic data interchange (EDI), errors can be avoided and processes cut out to reduce the total time. For example, Mazda redesigned the materials planning, purchasing, and accounts payable system through the extensive use of EDI to place orders with suppliers, and electronically log the progress, the receipt of goods and payment. The redesigned process reduced costs and improved speed and quality.

Again, EDI can be used to drive production processes. In the Midlands of England a highly regarded dyeworks, Stephensons Fashion Dyers Limited, used EDI to receive orders and to prepare recipes for dyeing garments as well as the usual tracking of orders, production and deliveries. This means that fashion garments can be produced in uncoloured form, dyed according to customer demand with a turnaround of one week and no risk of write-down due to obsolete coloured yarn. Previously, six weeks would have been more normal and Stephensons now have a real competitive advantage based jointly on IT and their undoubted technical expertise.

Marks & Spencer Plc (M&S) is famous for its retail formula success based on outstanding quality, value and depth of range. It has been able to reduce the initial margins on products yet enhance the margin after mark-downs by taking stock out of the system and responding much more quickly to changes in customer demand. To achieve this fast response, M&S work very closely with their suppliers in a real spirit of partnership for the benefit of customer, retailer and supplier. They have first-class information technology that really adds value within their business system.

The latest example is the 'contracts management system' that is being developed with input from major suppliers. It is a single paperless system that covers all aspects of how their buying groups plan, develop, issue and manage supplier contracts in response to actual sales trends in real time. The common database will be used by supplier and retailer capturing information once at source. Working practices will be largely screen-based, including the ability to use high-quality images for designs and the ability to store and use technical information.

Changes proposed with this system are profound. The basic document is the style file which contains the complete specification for the product from fabric, accessories, manufacturing instructions, sizing and pictorials of the finished product. This is the manufacturer's bible which also sets out quality standards and critical areas of quality acceptance. The present 16 000 style files in M&S, replicated in manufacturers, which hold full details of agreed specifications, may well change several times during the process. At present they are manually updated with potential for error. In addition to this there are thousands of contracts which are issued, progressed and altered when demand changes. There are thousands of communications and notes sent each month. All this will be replaced by the paperless single system which has the following commercial objectives:

- one-time entry of information at source;
- speed-up of product development time which is a major competitive advantage with fashion;
- reduce buying process costs;
- build closer supplier–retailer relationships;
- improve the visibility and control of the whole process by having a transport and supply chain critical path which would not be possible under the manual system;
- eliminate paper and the constant re-keying of data.

This is a transformational project that will deliver real value. It eliminates many business processes that do not add value and provides real value through additional shared information that helps managers to take time and cost out of the total process.

Managers must lead with IT

The purpose of this section is to reinforce the point that IT is a key area of added value for any business. It is regrettable that many managers still see this area as the domain of the boffin or where a specialist must take the lead. The simple fact is that IT is the responsibility of general managers who must champion the chosen initiatives. Any corporate strategy must be supported with an IT strategy and indeed in many cases IT will be capable of delivering a sustainable competitive advantage. As the service element is increasingly important it needs to be appropriately supported with IT.

Information systems have moved from the base level of simply processing transactions to a second level of providing decision-support systems. Many companies have moved to the third stage of strategic information systems that can help management plan the future for their company.

IT is about information management, moving from data to information that is relevant to management in their hierarchy of decisions. Increasingly, there are shared databases and knowledge bases deeply available in the organisation thanks to effective, growing communication networks. No manager can ignore IT or the management of information. There are positive competitive advantages to be secured which will enable the firm to deliver superior returns.

Managers also need to recognise that IT can prove to be a constraint to the speed of change, or worse still it can be the source of substantial losses if mis-managed. For example, in the case of a merger or take-over the integration of the business, with all of the expected benefits, may well be significantly delayed if there is insufficient high quality IT resource to provide the required systems. There are numerous practical examples of companies that have proceeded without appropriate time devoted to IT, leading to chaos, lack of control and financial loss.

Michael Earl, a consultant and author in this area, grabs attention at a seminar of general managers when he puts up the slide:

What have the following organisations got in common?

- The London Stock Exchange
- The Wessex Regional Health Authority
- The London Ambulance Service

(They all had a major information systems or information technology failure and the CEO had to go!)

Value from the centre

The first thing to observe is that the value ascribed to the Centre depends on whether the perspective is from that of a subsidiary or reporting division, or in contrast that of the group chief executive. There will inevitably be service areas that the group chief executive requires which may not always be popular. For example, the post-audit of significant previously agreed capital projects may not always be applauded by divisions as it lays bare their performance against their early expectations. Equally, flows of information for treasury, tax or fiscal reporting are likely to be more comprehensive than individual subsidiary companies would produce, thus creating extra work. Sometimes centralised purchasing may reduce individual companies' choice and this, too, can be resented.

However, if we try to take a total company view, the picture is often more balanced. First, in today's fast-moving world, there is great merit in having a fast speed of response from a nimble organisation. For me this means a decentralised management as a given so that decisions can be made as close as possible to the point of impact. If decisions are pushed down then it is helpful to have a statement of values as a guide to the overall culture of the company.

It follows then that the role at the Centre should exclude operating decisions of reporting companies so that centralised purchasing will not usually be appropriate. If there are gains to be made by grouping purchases for price reductions this is, in my experience, best achieved through consolidated price negotiation and decentralised purchasing. The individual company with the highest value of purchases is often best to take the lead on behalf of all others to achieve a price reduction or better credit terms. Networking is the key here, not central control.

The Centre should be staffed with outstanding people capable of adding value. However, there should be very few of them. As the large successful European company, Asea Brown Boveri found, there is little evidence that large numbers at the centre do anything other than slow down the process and add significant costs. Upon their amalgamation, the plethora of central jobs were wiped out and the 700-odd people either found a role in operations or left the company. Asea Brown Boveri are not the only major company to operate with a very small head office. Hanson Plc, the UK-based conglomerate with sales of £11 billion, have a small head office team of only around 90 people.

Significant role

There are areas where I believe the Centre must play a significant role. I believe these areas are strategy, structure (organisation and capital), people, significant projects, information and controls. A word or two about each.

As we have seen in the previous chapter, a corporation's strategy must be owned by the chief executive who will have played a pivotal part in its creation. The top-down group strategy must be centrally determined even though participation in the debate may be quite deep. This sets the framework for divisional strategies which must be supportive of the group's overall strategy. The Centre, with its wider views and more detached approach may well be able to add value to the subsidiary's strategies through proactive early input, challenging of assumptions and the resultant action benchmarks. The Centre must also commit to the resource side of the plan which evolves from the strategy.

Organisational structure is the enabling device by which the chief executive executes the plans of the company. It is really a central choice and not one that can be left to contributing divisions or subsidiaries. The choice between a geographically-led structure, a product-based structure, a business-led structure or some hybrid must be taken centrally. It will, of course, reflect the strategy as well as the strengths of the top team. Equally, the financial structure is a matter for the board. The balance between debt and equity with the various alternatives under each heading is, in my view, a matter best reserved for the board.

The development of people, succession planning and the deployment across the company is a key central area. Some training initiatives are best organised on a central basis and the chief executive will almost certainly wish to be involved in the senior divisional appointments to ensure cross-divisional moves are fully considered as a part of management development.

There will be centrally sponsored projects that cannot form part of any one individual division or subsidiary which can add real value. For example, the potential of airbags in motor vehicles was a centrally spotted opportunity at Coats Viyella and the initiative involved the fabrics division, the engineering division that works closely with the motor vehicle industry and the light stitching division. Other examples are readily available, including a national company like South African Breweries that had a number of divisions but was dependent on the South

African economy. A group-led initiative to look at overseas opportunities enabled an international presence to be taken up, interestingly enough, outside their core brewing area.

Information has two aspects:

1. The necessary flow to the centre for control and accounting purposes;
2. Broad information that can be fed back to divisions which may be of use in their trading.

This latter point has value where one division is very strong in overseas markets and can feed back trends to others or where different divisions serve similar customers with different products.

Controls are needed to monitor the progress of the group which should be a positive value-adding exercise. In fields of asset allocation choices need to be made to give the group shareholders the greatest value and this can only be carried out at the Centre. The challenge on major items of capital spend and the rigour with which the Centre appraises requests for capital spend will improve the thinking, the quality and the returns.

As chief executive of a major multiproduct, multigeographic company, I spend my time on value-creating exercises as follows:

*   strategy – group and division;
*   people – selection, development, succession planning, organisation;
*   team-building;
*   coaching to improve standards;
*   frequent site visits to understand business on the ground and to encourage initiatives or action. This too is an essential element of communication;
*   frequent customer contact;
*   controlling through budget negotiation, agreement, and measurement of the businesses against the agreed benchmarks.

These are the areas where it is judged that I can create greatest value. The survey of other general managers referred to in Chapter 1 has a very similar bias.

Can the board add value?

What can the board accomplish for its company? Responses range from 'it is the most important source of shareholder value' to 'very little, the directors go through the motions but add little except bureaucracy'.

A wider audience from the general public would also voice their suspicion that the non-executive directors of boards are all part of the gravy train of perks for the favoured few. Indeed, part of the current focus on corporate governance is based on concern because of the failure of some boards to act to avoid collapses caused by incompetence, dishonesty or a lack of strategic focus. This has brought pressure to examine both the composition and the role of the board with serious thinking on these issues promulgated through work such as that of the Cadbury Committee in the United Kingdom.

The question of how the board can add value is an important issue for each board to resolve individually. There is no homogeneous model of the board that will provide a universally perfect solution in each national or individual situation. Each company must also tailor-make its board for its own circumstances having regard for legal requirements, size and complexity, the stage in development and, importantly, having regard for the personality and defined roles of the Chairman and Chief Executive.

Perhaps the starting-point to finding how the board adds value is to dwell for a moment on the role of the board. There is a wide diversity of view about this. I have spoken to a number of directors in different countries who express disappointment in the quality of decision-making as well as the scope of the agenda. As one executive director described it: 'When I was elevated to the board I thought I had reached the pinnacle of decision-making. The reality was a huge disappointment for seldom was anything of real value discussed in depth and the contributions from non-executives was minimal.' At the other end of the scale is 'Joe Public' holding the view that the board is the super auditor, the body that protects shareholders' interests and the body that creates the long-term strategy. It seems clear to me that the latter expectation is unrealistic and even the most diligent, capable board could not satisfy such expectations.

An important contributor to help in this debate can be seen in one of the findings of the Cadbury Report in the United Kingdom where boards are required to consider and agree those items that are specifically reserved for board decision. Both the discussion itself and the debate over items reserved for the board's decision have added real value in the companies which have, to date, adopted this Cadbury requirement in the promulgated code.

A complementary part of this process of focus is also to dwell on the composition of the board and on an appraisal of its own effectiveness. Here the role of the chairman is crucial. Balance to give breadth of experience as well as detailed knowledge are hallmarks of a well-constituted board which today needs to deal with a faster pace of change, greater complexity and increased social obligations. There is a need therefore for a higher competence base achieved through better objective selection to the board, finite terms of office to refresh and of course training of directors. There are, in Europe for example, high-level but short board programmes like those run at IMD in Switzerland that provide direct focus on the role of the board. Greater utilisation of such programmes and the wider provision of board training would be very much welcomed by the business community and the public at large.

Where the board can add value

Against this backdrop, what are the areas where the board can really add value? It is suggested that there are five key roles which are of universal application.

1. The appointment of the chief executive

More than anything else, this decision will influence the future direction and performance of the company. Finding the right match of executive capabilities to the agreed strategic and operational priorities is very important. With this decision, the board expresses its vision of the company's future potential through the selection of the executive leader, ensuring a match between the skill base and the strategy.

2. The board's interface with corporate strategy

Nailing my colours to the mast, I, as chief executive, believe that it is my primary responsibility to propose a competitive strategy which, after board discussion and approval, I and my executive team must deliver. Is it realistic then, with all the pressures of time and complexity of business environment, to expect a meaningful contribution from the board on strategy? Yes, it is. Primarily through involvement in corporate strategy, the board can play a forward role by utilising the breadth of its experience. Indeed, it is argued strongly that the board must make its decisions within a framework of strategy – otherwise it resorts to *ad hoc* decision-making. Further, this involvement in corporate strategy prepares the board to deal with situations which might arise unexpectedly and need fast resolution.

3. The board as monitor of management

Clearly, to acquit itself of this role, sufficient relevant information must be provided and there will be an agreed spectrum of topics which will be brought to the board. These will range from financial monitoring, strategy execution, key appointments and organisational decisions as well as significant items such as the budget approval, major items of capital expenditure or major investments. The board must have sufficient information to monitor the health of the business.

4. Corporate accountability

The board must choose the external standards to which the corporation must respond, recognising not only its primary responsibility to share-holders but its wider role with the broader group of stakeholders. The role of an independent audit committee needs to be strengthened and their practice greatly improved as a first step forward of clarity and integrity. At present, where audit committees exist, they are often perfunctory and add very little of real value.

5. The agreed areas which have been specifically reserved for the board

These may well result in different lists for different companies. Most efficiently-run boards will have a predetermined list which will be regularly reviewed and sets out areas of decision-making that must come to the board.

Role of chairman

Last, but by no means least, we must reflect upon the role of the chairman because, more than anything else, the effectiveness of the board will depend upon how well the chairman acquits himself or herself of that role. The quality of the chairman's leadership is undoubtedly the single most important factor in determining the board's effectiveness and efficiency. The chairman's leadership will provide an atmosphere where the executive are monitored or challenged yet the board retains its unity. It will allow opportunity for the different rich experiences of the directors to be aired on relevant topics. The chairman will ensure that there is a balance between the commercial imperatives as the key driver and social responsibility rightly demanded in our modern age. Dealing with natural tensions in a productive way is meat and drink to the modern-day chairman.

Of course, even adopting these proposals does not provide a universal panacea. However, thoughtful consideration and debate of these issues will provide considerable value. There is considerable value for corporate boards to meet to discuss their role, to agree how they can add value and to monitor their own progress. Modern-day corporate governance calls for more talented non-executives on the board who are better trained and have more time to devote to the increasingly complex nature of their role and who are properly rewarded. Getting balance on the board is an essential first step requiring a professional approach to executive and non-executive recruitment alike. The corporate board has a critical role in both the modern society and in the individual business. It must not only provide real value in both arenas, but also be seen to be doing so to retain its relevance and impact in a fast-changing world.

Heart of management

Adding value is at the heart of management and this thought must pervade all managers' thinking and activities. The areas of greatest influence which have the most beneficial impact will order the priorities of the manager's time allocation. This chapter has dealt with a number of ways that value is created. Each topic is worthy of more detailed study in its own right. Equally, in other parts of this book the reader will be quick to spot additional opportunities.

8 Communication

Plan the programme

Communication is the blood that flows through the veins of any enterprise. If it ceases to flow there are serious consequences for the corporate body. As with most important things in business life, the process of communicating is enhanced if there is a clear understanding of the objective and of the process, coupled with skill in the delivery. This means that a manager needs to be clear what he or she wishes to communicate, the various vehicles which will be used and some objective feedback of how successful the programme actually is.

Many managers find it helpful to write down formally, at least for themselves, an integrated plan. It might look something like the suggestion in Figure 8.1.

Figure 8.1

---

1. **My main objective** To ensure that the company's vision and strategy are well understood, and presented in a clear, motivational way appropriate to the specific audience.

2. **Key messages:**

   External
   - Ensure that strategy is reinforced with a clear understanding that this implies infill acquisitions in the core business and gradual divestment in the non-core areas.
   - Seek to reinforce the positive attributes of the company's style and standards of high quality in all that it does. Emphasise the culture of openness, and of the need to raise standards, as a priority.

   Internal
   - Ensure that managers at each level of the hierarchy understand the strategy.
   - Promulgate the need to accept higher standards and perform to them.

- Present half-year and full-year results with appropriate underlying messages.
- Promote the company's statement of values.

3. **The following channels will be used:**

External
- At least once a year one-to-one meetings with key people – press and institutions. See analysts at least quarterly.
- Formal presentations twice a year of results and also when any major significant events take place.
- Arrange one major event for analysts' site visit or as a special 'focus' event.
- Annual report is a key document and must be to the highest standards.

Internal
- Use special Fastline for quick simultaneous reports to worldwide staff for key events and a quarterly update (target: middle and senior managers).
- Use company newspaper for more in-depth stories of the group to build knowledge and awareness (target: middle managers through to workforce).
- 'Briefing dinners' monthly for key managers (rotated to cover all target group in 12 months).
- Visit all worldwide key sites annually and others of significance at least three times a year.

Key dates and benchmarks
List key dates in the programme and any measurable objectives arising from the key messages.

Feedback will be obtained
- During the first quarter in externally conducted survey of management and staff attitudes to the company.
- Direct confidential feedback results from meetings with analysts, institutions and by the PR agency.
- Objective review of press coverage every six months.

Figure 8.1 Personal communications plan

In any good plan, the manager will need to measure his progress against the benchmarks and be flexible enough to make adjustments depending upon the feedback or lessons learnt.

How much?

An organisation will have specific needs at any time so that the emphasis will change. If there is a change in strategy it will be a priority to ensure that there is a common understanding with the appropriate amount of detail at different levels in the organisation, as well as externally. As a particular example, the management of change requires large doses of communication.

How much time should be spent communicating to ensure that the manager is oiling the wheels sufficiently? While the old adage that you can never communicate enough is a valuable truism, this is not much help to one trying to allocate time to priorities. The real answer is that the time allocated will certainly differ in organisations that are at different stages. It also depends on how you define the various general management tasks. On average, from personal international research which was highlighted in Chapter 1, we have seen that general managers claim to spend between 10 and 50 per cent of their time on communication. The great majority claim to spend around 20 per cent of their time in this area. The respondents were asked to allocate their time between strategy, controlling activities, maintaining external relationships, people development and others. Communication, both internally and externally, has a high priority, with the average time allocated estimated at around 20 per cent. It is therefore not surprising that when those same managers were asked to prioritise important characteristics of general managers, they rated ability to communicate as third most important, after leadership and personal drive/energy.

Ways and means

Much has been written about 'management by wandering around'. It is well-recorded in management literature as desirable and is a more memorable concept because of the suggestion of the haphazard dimension of wandering around. Experienced general managers know there is no substitute for seeing each important part of the company on the ground. It is instructional to see how managers perform in their work environment, how well they lead their team. Often a boss will draw conclusions of a manager's competence from brief meetings, perhaps at head office and probably when the manager is presenting. Judgements about competence or potential are often only based on this sort of contact. Equally, judgements may be made about individual businesses from reports and numbers alone. This is of course a poor substitute for having visited the site and seen the operation with its people at first hand. In addition, the visits to differing sites or places of work give an opportunity for the general manager to reinforce the culture or key messages – 'to walk the talk', as they say.

Successful general managers will take every opportunity they can to draw together various members of the team on differing sites to preach the key message with the appropriate level of detail. Taking people into your trust as well as your confidence by sharing important information directly is an essential ingredient of teambuilding. Because there is not enough time to see every remote part of a general manager's domain, especially when there are significant international dimensions, the personal direct contact must be supplemented by other vehicles of communication.

Many companies will utilise video-conferencing links increasingly for multisite communications, especially now that this is becoming much more cost-effective. Company videos sent simultaneously to all sites are used by many companies to communicate one-off messages or to comment on annual or half-year results. Some companies, like Grand Metropolitan, have utilised audio tapes for, say, a monthly message from the chief executive as managers will be able to listen to them in normally unproductive time, for example, while driving their car.

Internally, with use of IT facilities or even modern fax facilities, simultaneous written and pictorial messages can be flashed around the world in minutes. A chief executive can send his plea for better performance or his inspirational messages on a regular basis to a tightly defined audience. The company newspaper can be a great channel of communication. It is usually under-used as a tool because it is often not targeted at a particular audience, may often be prepared in an amateurish way and there may be confusion as to content. The social pages need to be just that and of interest to the majority of readers. The space for key messages of information need to be professionally presented to reinforce the points in the agreed strategy. The whole publication needs to be attractive and interesting to read.

The role of PR

The major objective of business public relations is to present the company in a favourable way to the major stakeholders but especially to the shareholders. This will involve having a clear communications strategy with a plan of implementation together with a package of initiatives that are supportive of the main aim.

There are two simple rules when choosing a team to help with public relations:

1. Choose people you trust and respect both for their professional ability and their integrity. They must feel able to give genuine feedback no matter how unpalatable this may sometimes be. Beheading the messenger is not acceptable corporate behaviour!
2. Choose people who would be persuasive and worthy advocates of your messages and who have the time and motivation to work to the company requirements.

Once chosen, the team's role is to help the company to communicate in a way which enables the target audience not only to understand the message but to support and endorse the message. Formulation of the message requires an intimate knowledge of the audience and how they will react to the messages. An audience will cruelly test for realism and consistency with the overall strategy or general expectations.

Improving presentation techniques

How often have you seen a really good manager present poorly? The impression that remains is of a bumbling, incompetent manager lacking in confidence and ability. There is a clear message to all managers. You have to be good, and be seen to be good. This means that each manager must develop presentation skills and an ability to present in public. These are skills that can, and must, be learnt. Further, because there is always room for improvement even the most polished presenter would do well to top up the skill base with coaching on a regular basis.

Surprisingly enough, many managers are myopic about their presentation techniques and do not see the absolute need to improve them. I would recommend that all managers should see themselves through the eyes of the audience which, thanks to video technology, is now available to all. It is humbling to see the peculiar, off-putting habits, the hesitating, the unfortunate mannerisms and the fidgeting that detract from the message.

Practical points

There are plenty of books on the topic and plenty of good courses in almost every country, so I do not propose to give a detailed account of hints about public performance. However, there are a few practical points that are worth remembering:

1. Know what simple, clear message you want to leave with the audience. This remains your central theme throughout the presentation.
2. Prepare your message well in advance. Research what the audience wants to hear before you prepare anything in detail. It is usually helpful to start with a rough or a schematic draft to get the skeleton right. Add in the examples and illustrations, to build up an integrated story that has memorability as well as interest.
3. Start strong and go straight to the point. You must capture attention right at the beginning.
4. Build your message remembering that the span of attention falls off after 10 minutes! You will need to 'involve' them personally.
5. Close in a memorable way.
   - The audience needs to remember your central message.
   - Summarise the key points.
   - Use an anecdote or illustration to have a dramatic effect.

Presentation tips

Now for a few useful tips on the way that the presentation is delivered to the audience:

- Dress appropriately to the occasion.
- Be careful about posture when delivering. Feet should be slightly apart with no bending of knees or sideways movements.
- Make sure your body language does not send the wrong messages.
- Make eye contact with the audience from left to centre to right to centre.
- Vary the tone of delivery, the pace and pitch at appropriate times to gain emphasis.

With this background there are the three Ps to remember:

● Prepare
● Plan
● Perfect

Finally, compare these tips with the five basic principles that Winston Churchill developed when writing his speeches. They are:

1. Have a strong opening.
2. Keep to one main theme.
3. Maintain simple language.
4. Use analogies.
5. Have an emotional ending.

Shareholder communication

Any publicly quoted company needs to think carefully about how it communicates with its key shareholders as well as how often it does so. It is certainly a foolish assumption to imagine that large shareholders can be ignored except when the company needs their backing for acquisitions, disposals or capital changes including rights issues. Today, in most developed countries, companies will have a clear investor-relations strategy including an annual plan of events. The chief executive, along with the finance director, certainly needs to allocate sufficient time to this priority. It is not always necessary to have a company investor-relations manager, especially if good quality outside help is available from specialists. However, it is increasingly important that large shareholders need to feel that they are a priority and that the effort of the top team is made willingly and not grudgingly.

The common base level of information is the regular reporting which is likely to be quarterly in the USA but in most cases half-yearly in other countries. Clear, open, full disclosure wins high marks from shareholders and increasingly the better companies are providing in-depth analysis of the financial performance. The best reports are easy to read, provide financial highlights in a conspicuous space, followed by the overview not only of geographic areas but also, separately, of the differing business streams within the company. The reports must be consistently written in a clear manner giving comment on the good and the disappointing points of the results and give a view about future conditions and the outlook.

Detailed numbers, useful to analysts because of their clarity and insights, should follow covering cash flow, profit and loss as well as the balance sheet. Both the interim and annual reports should also be seen as an exercise of involvement of shareholders, employees, customers and suppliers in the company. They must therefore be well-presented and serve this legitimate public relations exercise. This is a point to which I will return later.

At the time of the public announcement of the company results there must be formal presentations to analysts who represent the selling side (brokers or market makers) as well as to the buying side analysts who represent institutions. This latter group is increasingly important and also needs to be serviced with individual visits and discussions. The presentations will go through the results in depth looking beyond the formal financial reporting, and will include competitor comparisons, non-accounting measures and like-for-like performance excluding items such as exchange, non-trading gains, acquisitions and disposals. Typically, today, with British companies, institutional shareholders, both United Kingdom and overseas, will account for 80 per cent of a company's share capital with the top ten institutions accounting for perhaps 35 per cent of the total.

Shareholders, especially the institutions, will want to be clear about:

- strategy;
- the source of competitive advantage;
- customers, and how the company is serving them;
- competition, strengths and weaknesses;
- industry trends, new issues or opportunities;
- management depth, skills and structure;
- current trading conditions and prospects;
- a clear understanding of the numbers and what is behind them.

Marketing the company

Institutions are not all alike. They have different requirements, objectives and expectations. While some are looking for high income, others are looking for growth, some are national companies, others like an international spread of businesses with the resultant currency exposure. There are also those institutional investors, especially those in the USA, who look for 'value plays' where a stock looks undervalued. Others will look at counter-cyclical opportunities where the demand is weaker. In presenting itself to shareholders or would-be shareholders, it is necessary to know the different requirements and, to some degree, to tailor-make the individual presentation. The idea of repeatedly using the same generic material for different institutions that have different requirements is not helpful. It does not make them feel special, but rather devalued because time was not taken to prepare specifically for them.. We would never dream of doing this with our company products or services and should not when the company is presented to investors.

It really is important to get the balance right of presenting the company in a favourable light to prospective investors whose objectives are well-known, yet not to overdo this with glitzy marketing. When the job is done well, the rating will be optimal given the real performance expected and compared with the peer group or those competing for investor funds. Clearly, the higher the rating the greater the ability to tap the market cost-effectively for funds, provided of course that management recognise that this should only be done sparingly if a premium rating is to be maintained. Managers need to keep in the front of their minds that institutions are the only source of long-term equity capital.

Feedback from investors

A growing number of medium- to large-sized companies will often employ a firm of investor-relations advisors who will cover financial press relations as well as contact with analysts and institutions. They are well-placed to give continuous feedback on the company's performance in communicating and the perception of the 'City'. Almost invariably after each group presentation at both half year and full year the advisors will follow up on the day to glean feedback on investors' views of the following topics:

- results against expectations;
- key messages received from the presentations;
- standard of presentation;
- residual concerns;
- changes in expectations in ratings of buy, hold or sell.

All this adds up to the overall assessment of the company's future growth which is the key judgement that analysts and fund managers must make. The results are quite illuminating and because the respondents' replies are treated anonymously, the feedback is very direct. Usually, a clear message is received.

Equally, a similar follow-up from financial journalists will take place before publication to check that they are clear about the key messages and any doubts or concerns are dealt with either by executives or analysts, who are chosen because they are knowledgeable and empathetic to the company! When the articles are published, they should be read carefully both to learn lessons from the coverage and to check on the communication of the key messages.

Shareholder research

Increasingly, many companies are going further than this and will commission research, usually with institutions, to learn more about messages received or about their expectations. Not only does one need a well-thought-through questionnaire but the institution must grant access to the right person, the decision-maker in the sector. As with all market research, the appropriate base must be chosen to give a sample large enough and representative enough to draw valid conclusions.

Specialist research firms in this area would survey institutional shareholders accounting for around 25 per cent to 30 per cent of the shares in issue. The survey would include those shareholders that have an above-average shareholding and therefore are overweight (supporters), those that are average (neutral) and those that are underweight (agnostics). To be really useful, the research must not be taken in isolation but rather measured against the competition. it is perhaps helpful to take the competition not only from the same sector but to also select companies from within the industrial index. Not only is it important to get the sample size right, it is also critical to be able to talk to the right people in the individual institutions to ensure that the views expressed are from the power base where decisions are truly made. In other words, the research must establish the Institutional House view, and not just an off-the-cuff comment of an individual, perhaps junior member of their team.

Share prices, values and ratings are often emotive issues for a management and in many boardrooms there is a lack of common understanding of the factors affecting the particular company share price and its position relative to competitors. It is therefore instructive to present a comprehensive report to senior management and the board annually as a part of the investor-relations programme.

Investor-relations report

The annual investor-relations report to the board is an opportunity to see the company through the eyes of investors and is best presented by an external advisor to the company. This can be the investor-relations advisor, the broker or a specialist consultant. An objective, impartial view is needed if there is to be value in this exercise. Typically, such a report would cover the following key areas:

1. *Historical share price performance* compared with peer group and appropriate share index. This is coupled with the level of trading activity within the shares.
2. *Company performance* for the past four years and the consensus view for the next two years:

   • pre-tax profits;
   • earnings per share;
   • operational cash flow per share;
   • return on capital employed.

   All of these company measures will be contrasted with the peer group and wider indices comprising the relevant major part of the particular stock market where the shares are issued. In the UK, the non-financials group is often the relevant measure.
3. *Attitudes to the company* What do investors feel are the key issues or what are their concerns? This will cover comment on strategy, performance, financial position, management and industry or competitive issues. It will give a chance for investors' views about the outlook for the company and industry compared with other sectors or with the competition.
4. *Valuation* The current rating and the reasons behind this need to be explained. Implied earnings and dividend growth rates can be examined. Why does this company have the particular rating? Are the key positive and negative factors influencing an investment in the company? What are the investors' views of dividend policy compared with the company plan? Can we conclude from all this anything about investors' intentions?
5. *Changes in shareholdings* Who have been the buyers and the sellers and can we determine the reasons for these actions? For example, some institutions buy and sell entirely on perceived 'value' vis-à-vis other possible stock selections, while others will buy more on 'sentiment' or their subjective view of future prospects. It is always

worth formally listing the top 20 shareholders who will typically control 45–50 per cent of the company and see how this has changed over the reporting period.

6. *General conclusions* How is the company regarded and what is its standing in the financial market-place? What is the outlook and likely implication for the company share price? Are there any messages about expected financial performance compared with the competition that the company needs to take on board? For example, will future earnings growth and cash generation match or exceed the average opportunities available to investors? Is management's standing robust and is the investor-communication policy working?

These are important issues for the board which are not always properly addressed. I also strongly suggest that this is valuable, insightful information for the management of a listed company. It will help them to gain a better understanding of the company through the eyes of the shareholders who, after all, own the company. It is always useful to remind executives that they are there to serve shareholder interests as their priority! Therefore an investor-relations report may be aimed at the board of the company but will be shared with the deeper management to help them to appreciate the context in which they operate.

As with any presentation, it is important to present the results of research in an interesting and informative way, using graphs or visuals. Purely as an illustration, in Figures 8.2 and 8.3 I have included some examples using a fictitious company called Alpha. Figure 8.2 deals with Alpha's earnings growth, while Figure 8.3 explores the total return to shareholders. (The total return is the sum of dividends received and changes in the share price.) These examples illustrate some of the points raised in the investor-relations report.

The Annual Report

Here is an opportunity to provide a real window on the company, first and most importantly for the shareholders, but also to present the company to customers, suppliers, employees and the community. There are of course statutory requirements which become the base position. However, there is so much more that can be communicated through this vehicle to the stakeholders in the company. Historically, many companies have seen the annual report and accounts as a chore with the minimum of disclosure or forethought in making the report worthwhile. Then the annual report becomes a lost opportunity.

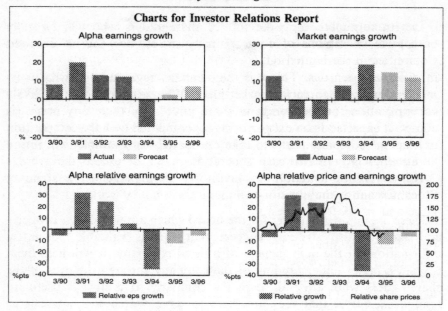

Figure 8.2   Alpha earnings growth

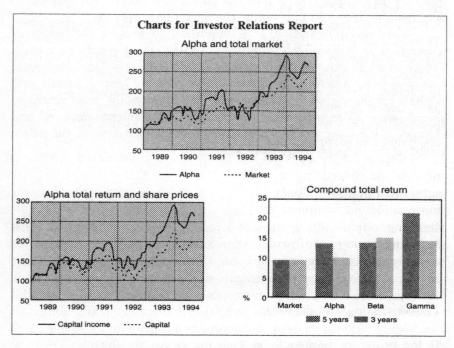

Figure 8.3   Alpha: total return to shareholders

Increasingly there is pressure for greater disclosure around the world both from champions of corporate governance such as the Cadbury Committee in the United Kingdom and of accounting standards boards in different countries. This is to be much applauded so that management's performance can be externally assessed and the health of the company better understood. There is more to be gained when the company sees this as an extension of its communication programme, and in keeping with good marketing practice preaches a consistent message in an attractively presented, clear way .

It is interesting to reflect on the approach of bodies such as the Joint Stock Exchange and Institute of Accountants who judged companies, large and small, for the best reports.

Although the detailed criteria by which the reports are judged are not published, a number of key factors are taken into account. Naturally enough, a proper observance of legal requirements and accounting standards is fundamental but this is really only the starting point. The winners amongst larger companies since the inception of this assessment include BOC Group, J. Sainsbury, Cadbury Schweppes and Coats Viyella. The judges also take into account positive qualities and features to be avoided which are shown in Figure 8.4.

Planning an annual report is similar to planning a marketing campaign. There is a need for early agreement on the theme, a plan of the detailed layout, a selection from alternatives of the creative approach that will work best, always remembering that continuity from previous years helps to reinforce the message. Today there is no place for the idea that you can have several people to write filler-text on aspects of the business to put between the photographs of staff, processes or products. This is boring, disjointed and inappropriate.

Producing the report is not just a creative task but also a production process which needs to be managed. If we get this perfected there are substantial sums of money to be saved through transferring financial information on computer disc, avoiding unnecessary alterations, and choosing carefully the paper quality and weight. Attention to detail including quality proof-reading is a necessary part of the process if the annual report is to be error-free.

Communicating with the workforce

If the power of improved performance is to be fully released in an organisation the total workforce must be more completely involved. This

Positive qualities

- Attractive, interesting and lucid presentation.
- Objective discussion and appraisal of the company's performance, financial position and prospects.
- A clear description of the company's business.
- Relevant financial highlights clearly and fairly presented.
- Relevant information about the board and its operations.
- Effective use of emphasis and design in setting out the financial information, including use of charts and diagrams.
- Prominent disclosure of relevant figures for each business segment tied into the narrative reporting.
- A clear five-year table of useful financial information.
- Clear information relevant to the individual shareholder.
- Inclusion of relevant ratios.
- Good disclosure on corporate governance.

Avoid

- Poor legibility from the use of small print or poor colour contrasts.
- Inadequate linkage between the accounts section and the rest of the report.
- Biased selection and presentation of key data in order to flatter performance.
- Relegation of segment details making information difficult to find.

Figure 8.4   Assessment of annual reports

requires good two-way communication with a desire to hear and act on the messages received. Needless to say, this needs an investment of time at the top and throughout the layers of management to ensure that corporate messages get through. One of the most frequently mentioned disappointments of top managers is that blockages to communication continue despite the time and effort invested. The commitment to communication must be complete and pervade the entire organisation.

(a)   What to communicate

To some extent, this will be prescribed by the nature of the company because a multi-product trans-national will layer its messages from top management to the workforce in a different way to a single product, single plant, national corporation. Therefore, top management must decide what to communicate and in what depth. Plant workers would like a very basic understanding of their group's strategy, more detail about their own company and much more knowledge about their own place of work. With this background I believe the following topics will be appropriate:

- Strategy, layered with increasing depth of knowledge of specific implications for the place of work.
- Key initiatives in the company and for the specific place of work.
- Changes in products, processes or key people.
- Performance of the company and the appropriate unit in terms that are applicable to the target audience. These will include sales, costs, profitability, cash generation, output, productivity, quality and customer or market measures.

(b)   How to communicate

Again, the choice will depend upon the nature of the company but the following channels are available and are used by successful managers:

- Site visits and meetings by senior managers, probably on a half-yearly basis.
- Team briefings within factories by appropriate unit, probably monthly.
- Within training programmes a slot should be included to update knowledge about the company or the group it belongs to.
- Internal media, with the company newspaper being the most frequently used. Videos are often used when a company is widespread. Newspapers, three or four issues per year, would seem appropriate and the video is usually an annual event.
- Management meetings with unions to keep them informed and to listen to the feedback that they provide.
- European works councils are now being tentatively explored by British companies in advance of potential European legislation. I believe that works councils set up with mutually agreed goals are an outstanding opportunity to improve communication with the work-force and to raise standards across the company.

There is no doubt in my mind that communication with the workforce will require greater effort and more time in the future. Managers will be clear about the key messages and will have well ordered programmes. They will hear and act on the feedback, helping to build trust as well as improve company performance. Managers will also need to sharpen up their communication techniques through appropriate training.

Summary

Communications permeate every aspect of the business. All managers, especially those leading teams, have been taught from the beginning to communicate, communicate and communicate again. It trips off the tongue so easily and, like motherhood, is unchallengeable. However, this is not enough for the general manager. He or she must allocate specific time for all aspects of upwards as well as downwards communication, internally as well as externally. The feedback loop is an essential part of the process to ensure that the right message is received, understood and acted upon. Many companies will ensure that they have an objective view of the success of their internal communications by having an external specialist to survey management and the workforce so that they can present a report. Communicating with the workforce is a demanding and a rewarding task. Successful managers will spend more time here, because they are increasingly recognising the pivotal role of the entire workforce in delivering competitive advantage that is sustainable in the long run.

General managers leading a business unit or corporation should not be too disappointed to find that their carefully honed message is not universally received immediately. While it might be frustrating, it is true that the communications programme needs to have a repetitive element to it because of the 'wear-out' factor of the message and the noise of other messages which may at times conflict. Any good communications programme will be layered, supportive and repeated appropriately at the different levels in the company. It will also make a legitimate use of 'theatre' in the process and encompass many different forms or channels. There will be full use of on-site visits, of video- or audio-taped messages, of seminars and presentation staff dinners, news briefings, factory-floor briefings and company newspapers. The key of course is to be clear what you want to communicate, select the appropriate channels and then to be consistent and frequent in the process.

9 Taking Charge

'It is with great pleasure and considerable terror that I stand before you today'. So goes the practised introduction to an after-dinner speech that goes on to describe the links of the speaker with the audience that give him such pleasure. The 'terror' arises because of the weight of the task coupled with the knowledge that there are such capable people surrounding him. These, I believe, are exactly the thoughts of first-time general managers as they approach the rather daunting task ahead of them. Indeed, it may perhaps provide a crumb of comfort to learn that these feelings never completely disappear as even experienced managers approach new challenges of new positions whether within the same company or beyond.

Stressful times

Taking charge is a stressful time for an executive: it is challenging, often daunting; hard work, but rewarding too. The longer each of us remains in a particular job the higher our personal comfort because of our familiarity with the key components of it. We know the people, the strengths and weaknesses of the team, direction is clear and there is a genuine familiarity with customers, product, processes and the value chain of the company. The problem about taking charge in a new situation is that you have to keep the business running while you learn about it. All around are expectant people waiting for early signs of direction or change so that there is an air of expectation of change. The new agenda will need to be exposed and the team converted to the action programme that inevitably follows. While the purist may argue that these are issues of leadership common to other aspects of general management, I believe there is real value in looking at the topic of taking charge as a separate focus because of its importance.

First appointment

I can easily remember my first real general management post – to run the publicly quoted Cadbury Schweppes South Africa group. Fortunately, I had two years prior experience as Commercial Director of Schweppes and Group Finance Director there so that the political–economic environment was not new. There were clear issues with the group which had performed very badly, largely because of the failure of the combined Schweppes–Pepsi Bottling Company to perform to expectations or any reasonable standards of performance. Indeed, this important part of the group was a loss-maker that hungrily used cash, starving the attractive confectionery business of funds.

With the benefit of hindsight, the issues were very clear:

- The strategy was not competitively based and would not deliver value because of the problems with bottling the drinks.
- The team lacked corporate leadership and the confectionery management were demoralised while the drinks management were out of their depth given the enormity of the task ahead of them.
- There were a myriad of operational issues that required resolution.

However, at the time, I was rather overawed at the task ahead and in a 'return to the womb'-type response, I endeavoured to look at the business through financial analysis. For me the business was underperforming and I looked through the differing facets of the numbers to get a good appreciation of where the problems resided and which areas held the greatest opportunities. While this produced some degree of enlightenment, the large number of options and issues clouded the simple fundamental messages. It was only when the broader strategic approach was taken, and quality time was spent with the key players, that a genuine directional understanding emerged. This conditioned response of returning to one's leading or primary discipline is not atypical of others entering general management for the first time.

In discussions with general managers about their first post, I have found that this reaction of returning to your primary discipline is a familiar approach. The Australian sales and marketing director appointed to his first general management post which was in the United Kingdom, reviewed the business through his sales and marketing eyes. He segmented the customers, talked about the products and services and went through the products and their position in the markets compared with competitors. While of course he had an understanding of the total numbers of his new business his point of entry was through market analysis, product profitability and product opportunities. In this instance, the new incumbent was a good choice for the general manager role as the company needed growth after a long period of cost-cutting and retrenchment.

Equivalent vignettes can be seen in the production field where the point of entry is often to focus on technical breakthroughs, cost-reduction or process improvement in the first stages. Perhaps more rare is the example of the Personnel executive who is elevated to general management. Yet again, here we see the familiar approach. As an example, J. & P. Coats took their divisional personnel director, who had latent general management potential, to manage a troublesome market in the Far East where the team was underperforming. This manager's sensitivity to cultural diversity, and his understanding of the key need to rebuild a balanced team of professionals were good reasons to make the appointment. There were issues of suboptimal market performance and a need to improve systems and controls which were well-recognised by the company and the new incumbent. Here, the manager's initial approach was through the area he knew best – approaching the key people, building a team together a common goal and enhancing capabilities. The specifics of concern in the business were dealt with as a second level.

Practical lessons

There are some observations from these examples. First, it is totally legitimate to approach the responsibility of taking charge through the discipline you know best. It is quick, relatively easy and you are less dependent on others to make judgements about what you have discovered. However, there are significant limitations to this approach. The very nature of the new task should remind us of the need to look more widely at the key factors, to evaluate the total value chain. This is especially important when there is a double dose of newness, first from the change in role and perhaps also from a change in industry. In these cases, external help is appropriate as consultants can and do contribute in the process. They will help to provide fresh insights, speed of analysis and an ally in conditioning the management team for change.

Dealing with consultants requires discipline and control. They will wish to carry out a full review, probably wider than the new general manager requires at this time. They will have in-house consulting products which are capable of providing value but may not be totally central to the immediate task. At the outset, it is essential to decide what your objectives are, and to make a study of what is involved at each sequential stage of work including the expected outturn. You need to agree the costs in advance too!

Sometimes, the process is expedited if the executive knows the consulting firm well and trusts their integrity. As an example, in dealing with strategy consultants whom I know well, I find it helpful to adopt a time-saving approach. Usually, I will have undertaken some fundamental analysis and drawn some tentative conclusions. The analysis is far from complete and may be partly flawed, as equally would be the conclusions. Then I will say, 'based on my preliminary analysis, I have developed the following prejudices', which I would list. We agree a work programme as described which will include testing the broad, tentative 'prejudices'. This avoids the wider task which consultants enjoy of surveying the entire field, putting forward choices, all brilliantly documented and presented under the guise of needing to have a full strategic review before looking at the specifics. My approach will only work if the consultant is challenging, independently minded and where the company has good analytic capability. The use of teams made up from company and consultant is a usual feature of value-added consultant contributions.

Other examples

In the USA, Jack Smith became General Motors' president in April 1992 having inherited a weak, malfunctioning company from Robert Stempel. Sales were slumping, stocks were excessive, efficiencies were poor and there was an organisational malaise. His story has recently been written up in *Fortune* magazine and, according to Alex Taylor III, Smith set his first goal as 'stop the bleeding' with a review of segmental sales, a new standardised approach to purchasing and avoiding expenditures on new model expenditures. His cost-cutting was remarkable and remains a legend in industry by reducing plants from five to three. He found the approach to make General Motors' assets more productive and gained economies of scale in engineering, production and marketing. These bold moves came with the confidence of 33 years in the industry and a deep belief in the need to move quickly.

His turnaround tips given to *Fortune* are as follows:

- Establish a vision for the whole company.
- Set clear expectations for performance at each level in the organisation.
- Construct realistic strategies that do not require rocket science.
- Develop the capability to execute by reorganising people and reallocating assets.
- Focus everything – all assets, all decisions – on your customers. They are the ultimate arbiters of success or failure.

This is a more direct approach where the learning phase was unnecessary because it was well-understood. He was appointed to make change and speed was of the essence. There are also other examples of managers from within taking charge at the top of the company with a mandate to change both style and measures of performance. Dominic Cadbury was appointed internally to the role of Chief Executive of Cadbury Schweppes Plc. He held a clear view of the things he wanted to do quickly because of his long experience in the group, much of it at senior levels. His speed of action was only tempered by the need to understand the drinks business fully as most of his previous experience had been on the confectionery side. His early actions were strategic by focusing the company on soft drinks and confectionery, having first sold off the distractions of the health and hygiene and foods business where it was clear that there was no real competitive advantage.

Change is inevitable

When a new leader takes charge, change inevitably follows. Sometimes, it is worth thinking about the source of change to have some idea of the likely emphasis that follows. It can occur through internal promotion when the new incumbent has a knowledge of the company and the industry. Here, the learning period is shortened and empirical evidence suggests that there is greater continuity so that change is more transitional. On the other hand, change can be thrust upon a company because it is clear from the evidence around it that existing strategies are not working.

Change can be injected from outside with a new externally appointed appointee who may even be new to the industry. In this case, it is usual to see a more radical form of change with fundamental challenges to the status quo.

Conditions for change

While the leader contemplating a new agenda will wish to involve and enthuse his team to achieve the change objectives, there is also the risk that they can be inhibitors of the programme. This is especially true if there appears to be a threat around their continuing role, a lack of understanding of goals or benefits. Therefore, any new manager anticipating a change programme needs to anticipate how the recipients of the programme will react and how to remove potential impediments.

This is an issue to which we will return later but, at this stage, I would observe that the task will be made much easier when:

- there is an unambiguous message clearly communicated and well understood by the receiver. The agenda must be short and focused.
- the strategic validity can be seen as appropriate and is fully endorsed by the board.
- the key message is reinforced by consistent behaviour that reminds individuals in the renewed organisation that new standards are essential. In other words, there is a motive of self-interest.
- non-supporters of the new agenda are clearly seen to have lost their power base followed by total removal if they are unable to support the team.

The positive aspect of people and change is that the challenge of change is exciting and stimulating for highly motivated executives. As they realise that they are empowered individuals who are responsible for their own destinies they can truly be a powerful source. There is a real sense of achievement as they make the journey and achieve the objectives for each milestone on the way. The scale will often excite and seldom daunt when tasks are broken down into manageable chunks. Coherence of the overall rational plan given an adjustable yet predictable path forward also provides a great stimulus.

It would be irresponsible to imagine that this happens without providing additional enablement for both management and the work-force. They must know more, through access to quality, relevant information, education across a broad front and through appropriate training. They will certainly be capable of doing more if supported by the right tools and resource and will do more when they are galvanised by motivation as well as incentives.

Overcoming resistance to change

We have seen that there can be blockages which prevent or slow-up change. Often the very people we strive to enlist into the change programme will feel threatened because of the new order of things and perhaps because they fear being a casualty of it. Even if the great majority of the management team have been embraced in the process, the speed of change can also be affected by passive or active resistance to it.

In my experience, resistance to change can be categorised into a number of broad areas. The first is where the real objective is not fully understood throughout the organisation. If there is no clear view of the destination it should not be surprising that the journey is not efficiently travelled. This leads to a lack of genuine commitment. Perhaps the key reason is insufficient or inappropriate communication leading to a lack of commitment. Early signs of this can be seen where top levels of management 'parrot' the outpourings of the boss without really understanding the implications or performance standards needed. On the other hand, there will be those detractors of the programme who dislike the upheaval change brings, finding it adds more work and brings into question their skill base which is needed to implement it. Here, we will see the 'shuffling feet' syndrome where key players will show all the outward signs of high activity while making little forward progress. This will be especially true if the participant thinks he may be working himself out of a job. We should not be surprised that in these cases the process takes more time! Perhaps the easiest example to deal with is where the lack of commitment is because sections of the management or workforce do not really believe that this programme will last. These participants must cooperate or leave quickly.

The second main reason is where the programme to implement change is not really integrated. Those on the receiving end collect a myriad of diverse messages and jump to the latest edict down the line. 'Death by a thousand initiatives' is the best description of this. As we all know, the change levers need to be supported with an integrated programme that is not complex and is focused on early big wins.

Third, there are genuine blockages which require management attention to ensure that the change programme can be managed to the expected time scale. An important example is the information management systems which are key to affecting change. To my own cost, I have found that far too often this determines the pace of change. Another example might well be in having unrealistic expectations from the change programme, especially early on in the process.

Fourth, it is very important to recognise the cultural diversity of a corporation and to be truly empathetic to this in working up the programme, especially with the communication of it. Many international companies will be multiproduct, across wide geography, with many different ethnic groups included. This is a situation which requires special attention.

Finally, we should check to see we have the appropriate leadership, especially at the top. The leader may have great insight to conceive of the change required but he needs to spell out his vision through clear communication and charge up his apostles to deliver the task. Anything less than this contributes towards potential failures.

Lessons from literature

Managers who have been through formal business education may well have a head start on their peers who have not. They will more quickly see the bigger picture and the key issues to focus on a short agenda of really important items. In the search for help from management literature it is regrettable that there is a dearth of good material focused on the concept of 'taking charge'.

An exception to this view is the work of John G. Gabarro of the Harvard Business School who has both studied this topic and undertaken research. In fact, he too supports the notion that little is known about the process of taking charge when he observes that it is one of the least understood activities in management. Gabarro, in his research, observes that the whole process takes up to three years depending upon the incumbent's ability, previous experience and the key nature of the task ahead. A tough turnaround requires more effort than a steady maintenance of the broadly acceptable status quo. His research also points to five stages which are clearly identifiable which require different forms of learning and which have different action outcomes.

First, he sees *taking hold*, which is a period of operational evaluative learning and with the outturn of corrective actions. This phase is typically three to six months but I would observe that the organisation will be restless if the first hundred days pass with no discernible action from the new manager who has taken charge.

Second, is a longer period of *immersion* which is reflective more than action-oriented as the key role here is maintenance and the preparation of plans for action in the next phase. The time for this phase will depend upon complexity for it is a period of penetrating learning, lasting between four and eleven months.

Third is *reshaping*. A period of major change when actions are taken based on the learning from the previous period. This is usually accompanied by significant organisational change and typically lasts from three to six months.

The fourth stage is one of *consolidation* which is an evaluative period of systematic feedback and adjustment lasting a year. The final stage is one of *refinement* which is putting the incremental learning into practice. Perhaps it can be seen as a time of maintenance or the 'lull before the storm' as in a fast-changing world new actions of a more fundamental nature will inevitably follow. However, it is certainly a time when the manager's additional learning from his experiences is used to refine the direction.

Leadership tips

As with most dimensions of general management, the role of leadership is of real importance when taking charge. The actual leadership role is an important factor for success, especially in change at the top of a company. Real competitive progress is only made when a strategy is created, clearly defined and communicated. This must then be coupled with the delivery of the potential of this strategy through committed, capable people who have been well prepared. The leadership perspective here is not about creating some super power in the organisation to whom all managers turn for corporate wisdom and decision. It is much more like a team agreeing a strategy for a season and the tactics for the game. The selection of the key players enabling them to use their skills and creativity within the strategic framework which they will need to know like the back of their hand is most important.

When the newly appointed general manager approaches the challenge of taking charge perhaps in a new environment, the focus should be on strategy, his leadership, the team, the customer and the culture with the common ideals that are needed. While the initial analysis may well be through one dimension of business, through the numbers, the marketplace, technical or people, there is a need for a wider perspective.

Practical steps

There are practical steps which need to be taken.

1. *Assimilate information* from a wide variety of sources. These may be external where it is surprising what you can learn from sources as varied as analysts' reports on the industry or the players in it, electronic databases, suppliers, customers and even past employees. Internal analysis needs to start with the routine but also to include new insights, perhaps using new segmentation or approaches like activity based costing.
2. *Evaluation* – sifting data into manageable bites of information. This will help us to map out the current situation and choose action points likely to give some big wins.
3. *The agenda for change* where the leader gains agreement on the actions, the priority of them and the responsibility for achievement. There may well be a chance to create a simple rallying call to signal the essence of the agenda such as 'going for growth' or 'seizing geographic opportunities'.

4. *Continuous feedback and adjustment*, the iterative process that needs to be managed to optimise the action plan. None of this is freestanding from the business. It will permeate each part which in ideal circumstances will be seamless from strategy to budget to personal objectives to public relations. The new troops will be looking early on for signs of the new direction or emphasis.

Causes of failure

Naturally enough, new managers in new roles are focused on success not failure. Still, it is worth looking at failures to see if there are lessons to be learnt which will avoid repeating the same learning experience. Gabarro observes from his empirical work that the two most common causes of failure to take charge were, first, the lack of relevant prior experience and, second, poor working relationships with key people. In my view, we also need to add two other factors that are the primary responsibility of the company. Too often, insufficient thought is given to understanding the requirements for the general manager post and little objective evaluation of candidates to match their skill base against the requirements is undertaken. There is a need for greater rigour here. Then, after being selected to take charge, the hapless candidate is given little by way of special training or help in this role. This was clearly spelled out in the opening chapter, where all but a very few general managers received any help or training prior to their first general management assignment. Some of the surveyed managers who claimed to have received some guidance, in reality had nothing of value. It is clear to me that on these first appointments it is valuable to have a mentor available. He should be experienced and approachable without being interfering. The general manager's role is often a lonely one and support needs to be sensitive but available.

A practical illustration which incorporates many of the points already made in this chapter is found in the case study that is shown in Figure 9.1. This has the added interest of a hostile take-over situation, bringing together two companies with differing cultures.

Surveyed managers approach

In the survey of successful general managers described in Chapter 1, the respondents were asked about their first role, on taking charge. What training did they receive prior to the appointment, and what practical

─────────── **Case Study 9.1** ───────────

On taking charge at Coats Viyella

Early in February 1991, Coats Viyella made a hostile bid for Tootal. This was about 100 days from the date of my appointment to Coats Viyella as its Group Chief Executive. This followed a period of uncertainty in both companies as initially the bid had been mutually agreed but was referred to the Monopolies and Mergers Commission which took almost a year to clear the bid subject to two small inconsequential conditions. Coats Viyella had built up a 29.9 per cent stake but during the almost two years that had elapsed the textile industry and Tootal's fortunes had deteriorated. Therefore, when the bid was cleared to proceed, Coats unsuccessfully tried to obtain the approval of the Tootal Board to a much lower price. This was rejected, resulting ultimately in the hostile bid. Also, during this time the Tootal top management team was changed, making them more vulnerable with new top leadership.

There then followed a bruising, acrimonious campaign which concluded when the contest was won by Coats Viyella. Within two days of the announcement of the successful bid the top management teams of both companies were brought together by the Chief Executive of Coats Viyella to hear about the plan for putting both businesses together and to learn how management would participate through a series of task force teams. These task forces, numbering 35 in total, were seen to be an important way of dealing with the problems and opportunities that would inevitably result from bringing together both businesses. Team members were chosen from both companies with each team having a clear brief which covered, for example, amalgamating operations in particular countries, production configurations, the total customer interface, distribution resource, accounting and administration, technical, research and development. These teams were seen as an important part of the integration process as well as yielding benefits of wider personal understanding for the participants whether they were from the Tootal or Coats background. Also, at this time, I, as Chief Executive, interviewed all the new senior people and talked about a broad structure that would be put in place. Our commitment to the management was that we would choose the best-qualified person for each role from all the candidates, irrespective of their company background. There would be absolute honesty about the future prospects for each person, including a fairly generous redundancy package where people were no longer required. This, of course, created some uncertainty and anxiety but in the following six weeks I interviewed more than 150 people so that I had a reasonable idea of the candidates within the organisation, thus ensuring that I could test the recommendations of my direct reports. We were therefore able to announce the detailed organisational structure within six weeks of this first meeting and, well within 90 days, all the significant posts were filled. Four years on, we are pleased with the people chosen who continue to perform well and turnover of this group of people has been very low. Certainly, they have managed their fair share of change! Further, the integration has been very successful from a financial viewpoint. The synergy benefits were achieved six months earlier than planned with financial benefits that were 50 per cent higher than originally predicted.

An additional feature of this example is the fact that I had two separate slots of 100 days to effect major change. The first was upon my appointment to the new role when it was clear that resolving the Tootal situation was a particularly important issue. The whole management team was galvanised to achieve a satisfactory solution to this. The second was immediately upon acquisition of Tootal which provided 100 days to make substantial progress with the integration and reshaping of the Group. Reflecting back, the power of the teams was truly impressive and the team members' personal learning extended beyond situational understanding. Their growth also included personal development as well as building some early, valuable networking links that strengthened in later years.

help did they receive upon assuming the new role? Less than 7 per cent of the managers surveyed had good to comprehensive training while 9 per cent received some, but the great majority at 84 per cent received absolutely none!

Contrasting with this almost 90 per cent of the sample believed that formal general management training is desirable as a forerunner to the first appointment. The small number who did not see such value believed that picking up experience was a more important learning approach especially if there was occasional access to a mentor. There is a small body of opinion which treats formal business learning as unnecessary or helpful, but fortunately this is in the minority. One dissident to the notion of a formal programme of learning prior to the first appointment emphatically recorded 'No – not helpful, as management is an art, not a science'!

When it came to identifying areas for a top-up of knowledge, or for a focus of attention there was a wide array of topics where it was felt that formal training could be given. A number of respondees gave more than one area of attention that led to the following list in order of frequency mentioned:

- MBA, or a shorter Advanced Business Programme;
- Agree a formal in-house specific training programme tailored to the individual needs;
- Short fill-in programmes, especially in finance and marketing;
- Strategy, and aspects of leadership.

While the relatively low ranking of strategy may seem surprising given the importance of this in a general management role it is a reflection of the relatively high percentage of the sample who have either an MBA degree or have attended an Advanced Business Programme. In total, 55 per cent of the sample have either an MBA or attended a recognised Advanced Business Programme, in addition to their primary degree.

The approach that these new managers took to their role undoubtedly reflected the needs of the company, and the managers' past experiences. However about 40 per cent of the surveyed managers recognised that the first thing they needed to do was to listen and learn before making decisions. The ability to listen is, of course, an important strength, especially when accompanied by judgement to evaluate what information is being provided during this phase.

To give a flavour of some of the responses one manager whose preparation was the completion of an MBA degree some eight years previously stated, 'Within the first two months I had briefings from department heads and an intensive familiarisation period before I took any actions.' Another in a financial products company, took a similar approach by 'establishing existing performance both financially and of the incumbent management team. The existing management were asked to express their current objectives and how they were going to achieve them.'

Where an appointee is from outside the particular industry there is the added preparation of understanding the nature of the industry and the business levers that are important to drive satisfactory performance. This was reflected in the replies of those transferring to new industries. 'I had to go through a crash course of reading to immerse myself in this new industry and to understand my new company. A review of press articles and of current analysts reports was a most helpful introduction which was essential prior to my arrival, to establish credibility with my direct reports.'

Once the sample managers were satisfied with their initial level of knowledge their first significant actions taken fell principally into three clear-cut categories, which are listed in frequency of response:

	%
Strategy review	48
Organisational changes	28
Business reviews/improve performance	18
Others	6

Others, recognising specific needs in their business had special focuses, such as 're-presentation of the company's major brand, which had lost its way'. In this case the newly appointed general manager was an internal appointment from the marketing department. Either his appointment was made because of the specific needs of that New Zealand company, or perhaps because of his training in marketing.

It was clear both from the survey, and in the follow-up discussions, that the managers taking charge for the first time were conscious of the need for change, for this was, in the majority of cases, explicit in the appointment. Actions to demonstrate the directions of change were seen in the shifts of strategy and of organisational or people changes which were made quite early on. Perhaps, with the benefit of hindsight the time allocated initially to communication through the early stages when assuming the general management role, were underestimated: 'I never realised just how time consuming the communications task was, and just how critical this was to achieving early success', commented a British manager undertaking both strategic and organisational charge.

From a different viewpoint, a senior manager in a large, British conglomerate-styled company which had installed a new chief executive who was trying to reshape the group, saw things differently from his new leader. 'The new chief executive is not really effective in communication. We hear nothing for quite long periods, we do not talk openly about issues but, without warning, he will communicate downwards a new direction or set of plans. His management group wish they were at least consulted and listened to so that we could better understand the rationale for his decisions'. Regrettably, this manager's experience is not unusual as a number of managers at the top still see communication only as a top-down process.

One of the surveyed managers drew attention to the importance of building a team at this time. He argued that this was his most important priority, given the situation that was inherited. Team building is of course an essential element for success. It requires patience and time, but above all else a common understanding of the goal and the proposed pathway towards it.

Whatever approach is chosen by a new general manager he needs a goal and a short agenda of major objectives which he and his team need to achieve together. Adherence to this agenda will require skill and consistency if the objective is to be achieved.

Exciting time

Taking charge is one of the most important transitions that a manager takes, presenting an opportunity for personal growth with the ever-attendant risk of reputation damage in the event of partial or complete failure. It is highly individual, tackled in different ways by different people reflecting their style, strength and knowledge base. The needs of the particular situation also have a significant influence in events.

Taking charge is an exciting time for the incumbent as well as the company concerned. It is a time when fresh ideas can be tested, when step changes, in strategy as well as performance, can be achieved. There is an early window of opportunity, perhaps three months for the new leader to make his mark. All the answers will not be known at this time and it is therefore sufficient to signal a new style and intent. The message will need to get to all levels of the organisation quickly and clearly. While it would be easy to be overawed by the magnitude of the twin tasks of learning about the new environment and the organisation including its people, there is some comfort in prior experience coupled with common sense. The leader's opening agenda will reflect the priorities which will cover current performance plus strategy. The opportunity of focusing on areas where a major step forward may be made will not escape the new leader. He will find some comfort from Gabarro's study which puts a realism around the time frame. Taking charge requires high energy levels with deep commitment to success. It will be busy, stimulating and regarding – never dull or quiet. But then, whoever wanted a quiet life?

10 The Numbers

The starting-point

Numbers, numbers, everywhere you look there are numbers. The key is to be clear about those of greatest relevance. The purpose of this chapter is to help managers to have a basic understanding of those numbers that are important in business. Of course, if we were to cover in a detailed way all the numbers that one bumps into in a management career, then we would need a separate, comprehensive book on this topic alone. This chapter does not attempt to provide an introduction to finance for non-financial managers, for this coverage is readily available both in literature and management seminars. However, the goal of this chapter is to bring managers' attention to areas where they should have a good working knowledge of what is involved. The bias is very practical, based on numbers that make a difference and those that will be a help in achieving better decisions. Some of the concepts are relatively easy to follow while others in this chapter are more difficult. Both sets are important, even though it is not the purpose of this chapter to turn the reader into an instant expert in any of the fields. Rather, the goal is to create awareness of concepts that are important to successful management.

First, we cover external reporting and the pitfalls in reading these simplistically. There is also a special emphasis on cash flow which is the life-blood of any business. Reports to the board by managers on a business unit will often reflect the grasp of the manager of his area of control. The example used in this chapter is suitable for sharing with a business unit's management to plot progress against agreed benchmarks. The next section deals with financial and non-financial measures of performance as well as the all-important use of discounted cash-flow techniques for decision-making. This is important.

Turning now to the numbers themselves, perhaps the starting-point should be with the reported annual accounts because nearly every manager will have some contact with them. Surely these are a firm foundation on which the manager can rely. Yet, if this is so, why is it that there are a number of companies that apparently have healthy accounts and good financial progress, only to be exposed in the next time frame as insolvent?

156

External reports

Perhaps the great majority of managers work for a company that has to produce audited accounts. Certainly, most will examine this public information for competitive purposes or understanding more fully suppliers and customers. They will also use their own company numbers to explain progress internally. Therefore it is necessary to understand the key elements. Traditionally, the initial focus has been on the profit and loss account and in particular on the earnings per share line. Because these accounts were regularly audited a security blanket seemed to cocoon the financial probity of the company. Even company analysts in the past paid a great deal of attention to growth of earnings per share as a prime measure of progress.

Sometimes unreliable

However, it became clear, partly because of unpredicted company failures, some of which were spectacular, that reliance on the audited profit and loss account was a dangerous starting-point. This was because of the many different treatments allowed by the financial watchdog bodies around the world leaving the choice to individual companies. In the United Kingdom, Terry Smith highlighted in his book *Accounting for Growth* many different accounting practices which were typically used to give a rosy view of a company's progress. It would be true to say that many of these 'profit-stretching' accounting techniques were not widely endorsed or appreciated!

There were numerous practices of taking profits in the profit and loss account with much-less-obvious offsetting or sometimes larger charge to reserves. There were difficult-to-find examples of expenses being charged to reserves then later written off or indeed where liabilities were never recorded because of 'off-balance-sheet techniques'. Acquisition accounting gave great flexibility with write-offs of goodwill or pre-acquisition provisions for restructuring that were interpreted very liberally giving the new merged firm a flying start through the gradual use of the reserves. The 'fair value' adjustments were also abused by unrealistically charging adjustments not directly related to the acquisition such as the knock-on effects on existing standards. Often these adjustments would be made gross and not reduced by a deferred tax adjustment which has the effect of reducing the tax charge in future years giving a mismatch of timing and presentation.

Perhaps the final area where judgements are required is the expected life of assets or the holding value of investments. As an example, take the effective life of aircraft being leased thus influencing depreciation charges or as another example, the value of unlisted investments held by the holding company. Recently, in the United Kingdom, the retail grocery industry has changed its view about the value and life of supermarket sites. Previously, the high costs of development, including accumulated interest costs, would be capitalised and no depreciation written off the buildings on the assumption that if these assets were properly maintained they would not diminish in value. The problem was that the assets were single-purpose and inevitably, over say a 25-year term, socio-demographic factors may mitigate against continuing on the site. Valuers were not much help when they would often value on an ongoing purpose basis at a level that was double the estimated resale value. Argyll Group took the lead by announcing it was in future going to provide for depreciation as an annual charge and set out a very credible basis for doing so. This reduced annual pre-tax profits by 10 per cent but of course had no effect on cash generation. Argyll's competitors took different views with some doing very little while others took a substantial up-front charge as an exceptional non-trading item, thus significantly reducing the annual charge for depreciation. The financial market did not recognise that this had little impact on the cash generation of the businesses or shareholder value, but marked down share prices by varying amounts because of their simple focus on the profit and loss account, and the resultant preoccupation with earnings per share.

Different standards

Freedom of accounting treatment is now much more limited because of the worldwide trend of new, prescribed accounting standards. Basically, more detail is provided for analysts to get behind the numbers and even unusual transactions will flow through the profit and loss account including goodwill written off, provisions for integration and items previously deemed 'extraordinary'. This means that those using the accounts need to dig behind the numbers to get an understanding of how they are made up but at least there is more information available to the serious reader.

Inevitably, in a situation where unexpected failures surface without any apparent precursor to this in historical accounts, there is a temptation to blame the auditors. Usually the key motivation is that they are seen to have deep pockets rather than any genuine feeling of complicity or widespread incompetence. However, large awards against auditors have been made and in some cases it is clear, with the benefit of hindsight, they did not always use good judgement or employ good practice. In keeping with the environment, the awards have typically been much higher, perhaps unrealistically higher in the jurisdiction of the USA. Consequently, auditors are now seriously considering limited liability to protect the partners against potential bankruptcy.

Unable to rely on auditor

The key lesson from all this is that a manager cannot and must not rely on the auditor to ensure the accuracy or integrity of the company accounts. First, the auditors' responsibility is to the shareholders of the company for whom they conduct the audit. There is no guarantee that they will have discovered any fraud nor any reason why outsiders should place full reliance on them. The simple truth is that financial probity rests with the management of the company and, in the final analysis, the accounts must be the responsibility of the board of directors. Many of the best managements in leading companies are taking steps to ensure that they look in depth at internal control in a standard way. Each reporting unit's management is asked to sign a standard form which is replicated in all business units through the organisation so that the group chief executive and finance director can take a total view for the total group. This will then be reported to the board annually. An example of an internal control report which must be signed off by the managing director and the finance director of each individual company consolidated in a group is shown in Figure 10.1.

Key external reports

Profit and loss account

The annual accounts are the starting-point. The profit and loss account is usually the first stop of most readers, despite the limitations already discussed. There is no alternative but to spend time analysing what is behind the numbers by reading each line carefully, referring to the notes to the accounts and the text of the chairman's report and chief executive's

Statement by the Managing and Finance Directors of:

Unit/company   . . . .

At the year end and subject to the exceptions explained in a separate commentary:

1. The Management Returns (MRs) for the year end were prepared on the basis of a fully extracted and extended trial balance from the general ledger, including appropriate provision for accruals and prepayments, and comprehensive cut-off procedures.

2. A full stocktake was performed at year end and the valuation thereof was reconciled to both the detailed stock records and/or the book (financial) stock. Significant variances were fully investigated and appropriate adjustments made.

3. Adequate but not excessive provision was made for stock obsolescence on a reliable and systematic basis, consistent with that adopted at the year end.

4. Adequate but not excessive provision was made for bad and doubtful debts on a reliable and systematic basis, consistent with that adopted at the year end.

5. All inter-company balances were fully reconciled with corresponding company units balances, differences fully investigated and appropriate adjustments made.

6. All key control accounts were fully reconciled and appropriate adjustments made.

7. All suspense accounts were fully analysed/reconciled and appropriate adjustments made.

Managing Director   . . . .   Signed: . . . .

Financial Director   . . . .   Signed: . . . .

                                                          Dated: . . . .

Figure 10.1   Accounting controls checklist

report. A manager wishing to get a bird's-eye view of a target company may well find it valuable to dig out analysts' current reports from the company broker and one other house that follows the company. Both the annual reports and analysts' reports will segment the company by geography and product group as well as provide a five-year summary. In the latter case care must be taken to ensure that the comparisons are valid on a consistent basis and are not biased by one-off events. When changes have occurred in the current year then it will be necessary to adjust the previous year's comparisons to ensure that these are on a consistent basis.

Balance sheet

Typically, the profit and loss is followed by the balance sheet which describes in financial terms the assets and liabilities at the end of the year. Managers will need to establish the basis by which assets are valued, on an historical cost basis, although revaluations of fixed assets may well have been included. The balance sheet may include intangible items like goodwill, brands, patents or leasehold premiums. In USA these intangibles are depreciated yet in many other countries the value is left untouched on the balance sheet. Perhaps more controversially, brand values have been included as an intangible asset which is not depreciated provided that in the director's opinion there has been no permanent diminution in value. Some companies like Cadbury Schweppes Plc only include brand values for new brands acquired while others have included an assessment of brand value to build up the asset side of the balance sheet. In some cases, like Grand Metropolitan, the figures for intangibles are large, accounting for almost 80 per cent of shareholder funds or 40 per cent of the total assets.

There are also other areas that influence the accounts, especially where relative performance is being measured. Perhaps the most common area is the valuation of stock which can influence both the profit and loss account as well as the balance sheet. Most companies would use a consistent basis so that comparisons between years are valid. However, they may choose from the first in, first out method (FIFO), last in, first out method (LIFO) or the average. The impact of each method affects the profit and loss account and the balance sheet differently. Taking as an example a period of rising costs, the impact would be as follows:

FIFO   The profit and loss account is charged with the costs of stock on an historic basis which means the cheapest stock being used first. The balance sheet will reflect the more recent highly priced stock increasing stock values.

LIFO   The profit and loss account is charged with the more expensive costs of stock in the current period, reducing the current year profits. The balance sheet will reflect a low value which will often be unrealistic in regard to current replacement costs.

Average value   An average of stock costs in both the profit and loss account as well as the balance sheet. This is a middle course between FIFO and LIFO.

Special attention should be paid to changes in the basis of stock valuation so that the readers of the accounts can understand the impact on current year profits. While talking of changes, accounts readers should scan the notes to accounts to understand any other changes in accounting policy such as the rate of depreciation. These issues are not always highlighted!

The manager must also be aware of any liabilities (and assets) not actually included on the balance sheet, for example, commercial lease arrangements or contingent liabilities mentioned in the detailed notes. Again, with the balance sheet, the accounting policies and notes to accounts need to be scrutinised to ensure that the reader has gained a full understanding. Readers of accounts must also be aware of the implications of these treatments, especially on key ratios such as the debt/equity ratio when comparisons are made across differing businesses.

Cash flow statement

Lastly and most importantly, is the cash flow statement which for me is the key document. It is key because:

1. Cash flow accounting is less susceptible to different treatments;
2. The reader can see with great clarity the business transactions;
3. It is cash generation that determines the real value of a business.

This latter point is something to which we will return later. However, all general managers will need to ensure that they fully understand the implications of special year end initiatives to reduce the net working capital which does not always reflect the reality of average practice during the year. In practice, the cash flow statements for United Kingdom Plc companies are of variable clarity. Personally, I find it valuable to reorganise the cash flows in a summary form which shows the fundamentals with clarity. This is illustrated in Figure 10.2.

Ratios are also important and often included in the annual report and would include:

- margin on sales (operating profit divided by sales)
- asset turn (sales divided by operating assets)
- return on capital employed (operating profit divided by average capital employed)
- interest cover (the number of times interest payments are covered by profits before interest and tax)

	This year £m	Last year £m
Operating profit	100	80
Depreciation	41	37
Working capital	(24)	(18)
Reorganisation costs	(5)	(5)
Net cash (outflow)/inflow from operating activities	112	94
Capital expenditure	(55)	(45)
Sale of fixed assets	5	7
Interest paid	(21)	(24)
Taxation paid	(30)	(24)
Dividends and minority	(24)	(20)
Reorganisation exchange and other	10	5
Net cash flow	(3)	(7)
Acquisitions	(55)	–
Disposals	30	–
Change in borrowings	(28)	(7)

( ) indicates cash outflow

Figure 10.2 Cash flow

- debt to equity (total debt expressed as a percentage of total assets)
- earnings per share
- return on equity
- dividend cover
- net asset value per share

Reports to the board

Managers may wish to look afresh at the financial reports to the board of directors to ensure that clear and meaningful information is available in an appropriate time frame, without creating overload by including trivial data. 'Exception reporting', by highlighting significant performance variation from expectations, usually the budget, helps to create a climate of focus and understanding. Depending on the needs of the readers, visual presentation through appropriate graphs and diagrams will be an effective aid to clarity.

Financial reports will typically include the following:

- *Sales* with analysis of trends by major product group and geographic area. The underlying trend is the important message to convey, especially if the headline numbers are affected by currency changes, acquisitions or disposals.
- *Profit performance*
  1. Total company in the form of the statutory accounts
  2. Management accounts by major grouping
  These reports would normally include operating profits and margins, ratios and exception reports.
- *Cash flow performance* for the total company and then broken down by major group. Operational cash flow (i.e. profit before interest and tax plus depreciation) as a percentage of sales is also a useful ratio here.
- *Total assets* split by fixed assets and net working capital, by major division and for the company. This then enables the return on operating assets to be included.

The reports are helped by relevant charts and trend analysis and almost without exception will compare performance against the budget and the forecast, if there has been an update during the year, as well as comparing with last year. Once again, trends are important so that 'like for like' figures are needed to remove distortion.

Performance review

At least once a quarter I believe it is helpful to a board to receive a brief performance review for the company as a whole. This is best prepared on a cumulative basis as it is more of a trend statement than a monthly report. As can be seen by Figure 10.3, it covers key financial areas relevant to the company.

Especially valuable is the inclusion of external factors to help the board to reflect on the company's relative rating and reasons behind this. Under the heading of 'other financials' I have referred to the very important

Cumulative for the quarter ending . . . .

	This Year	*Budget*	*Last Year*

1. *Headline numbers*
   Sales
   Operating profit
   Pre-tax profits
   Operational cash flow
   Operating assets
   Total borrowings
   Total employees (000s)

2. *Additional data*
   Working capital
   Fixed assets
   Capital expenditure

3. *Key ratios*
   Cash flow per cent of sales
   Margin
   Working capital (weeks)
   Asset turn
   Return on operating assets
   Earnings per share
   Interest cover
   Debt to equity
   Sales per employee
   Added value per employee

4. *External financials*
   Share price
   Price/Earnings ratio
   Dividend yield
   Share price relative
   Market capitalisation

5. *Other financial*
   Debt rating
   Average cost of debt
   Average cost of capital

6. *Brief comments*

Figure 10.3 Company performance

concept of the cost of capital which must be fully understood if a company is to make incremental progress through marginal investment decisions. The calculation of the cost of capital is not always straightforward although the concept is simple, being the risk-free rate plus a risk premium that is appropriate to the company. This deals with the equity portion of capital employed and this will have the cost of debt factored in according to the company's gearing policy. We will return to this later.

Management information

In many companies, both large and small, there is a lot of data around, often distributed to different parts of the business. There are plenty of examples where much of this data is unusable as it needs further refinement or to be drawn together in a meaningful way. Management need relevant information that will help them in their decision-making on time.

As can be seen from Case Study 10.1 (from the files of Touche Ross) it need not be a complex or difficult task to rearrange existing data in a more meaningful way. The resultant accounting system supported management in making decisions such as make or buy and helped forward the planning of capacity as well as providing relevant control data. The company improved productivity lowered costs and raised profits as a result of this focus.

Financial knowledge for managers

Managers must be familiar with the reports and concepts already mentioned. They will need to have much more information about the areas that they manage which will vary according to their role. This means that managers must be clear about what is relevant for the appropriate management of their constituency. The reports will include financial and non-financial areas and will cover operational performance as well as strategic. Most executive information systems give managers the facility to overview information with the use of colour on the screen to highlight exceptions and then to drill down to the level of detail desired. This is an efficient way to access the data which is increasingly being held on a common database.

Case Study 10.1

Touche Ross and a capital goods manufacturer

The company is a capital goods manufacturer, engaged in three principal activities:

- the manufacture and sale of lathes to industrial clients;
- the manufacture and sale of spare parts for such lathes;
- the sale of subcontract turning services and the renting of lathes.

At the time of the assignment the company was growing rapidly with demand from new overseas markets putting pressure on UK manufacturing capacity. The directors were keen to identify ways of improving manufacturing efficiency so that rising demand could be met and to establish a framework for both tactical and strategic decision-making.

Two examples of decisions which at that outset were being made on 'gut feeling' and little else were:

- the 'make or buy' decisions, i.e. whether to manufacture components within the company or to subcontract them;
- decisions concerning the timing of new plant acquisition.

Whilst the company was well-established, the management team at the time of the assignment had arrived as a result of a 'management buy-in'. Although a complex series of databases had been developed to record, for example, operator timesheets, contract details, purchase orders and product specifications, little information was available to support key management decisions. The major deficiencies in the database system were:

- the absence of simple controls (such as periodic reconciliation of related data) to ensure the integrity of the information;
- the way in which the information was presented. For example, there were no reports available to enable operating performance to be measured.

Touche Ross designed a monthly reporting package using information obtained from the existing database system.

- data collection procedures were improved and periodic reconciliation of timesheets to the payroll was instituted
- the monthly reporting package included the derivation of marginal rates – key information in deciding whether to make or buy components.

The final product of the accountant's work was a consolidated management report which included:

- direct labour performance measures such as:
  1. utilisation – a measure of the amount of useful work done
  2. efficiency – a measure of labour performance related to standard times
- a cost analysis which enabled movements in the marginal and fully absorbed costs of production to be monitored
- a forward load analysis; comparing the available capacity, in terms of machines and direct labour hours, with the forecast demand for production.

As a result of the above, management were able to forecast the capacity requirements for machines and, in conjunction with the derived costing information, decide upon the most appropriate course of action, either to:

- increase the availability of machines by changing shift patterns
- subcontract that work which was in excess of capacity, where such services could be procured for less than the marginal rate
- rank the tasks to be subcontracted to optimise profitability.

(with permission of Touche Ross)

Discounted cash flow

There are some additional concepts that need to be appreciated by managers if they are to understand in full the value drivers in a business. The first is the use of *discounted cash flow techniques* (DCF). There are many excellent, detailed treatments of this and related subjects so that it is only the key principles that will be addressed here. Forecasts of future cash flows expected will be appropriately discounted according to time and by the cost of capital, adjusting for inflation and risk, after which a residual value is added to take into account the value at the end of the time frame analysed, resulting in a *net present value*. This approach is appropriate for determining the financial viability of new projects including acquisitions. When evaluating capital projects the same approach may be used but then the cash flows will be interrogated to give a pay back in years and an internal rate of return expressed in percentage terms, that can be compared with the cost of capital. While most managers will be able to undertake simple DCF calculations on almost any one of the many software packages, it is perhaps more important to be able to test the assumptions and to pursue some 'what if?' alternatives through sensitivity analysis.

Questions managers may well ask will cover the following areas:

- Testing the timing of outward cash flow for the project as this has a major effect.
- Checking the business assumptions leading to the revenue projections included in the cash flows. How realistic are these? Have competitor reactions been included?
- Cost assumptions need to be tested for realism, especially timing implications of one-off payments (say for advertising) that will build revenue in later periods.
- The effect of disruption.
- Are the assumptions about residual values realistic and appropriate?

Cost of capital

The cost of capital is of importance as any business that earns less than its cost of capital is going backwards. Regrettably, the calculation of the cost of capital is not always straightforward or universally agreed. For those who wish to gain an understanding in depth I suggest they read McTaggart, Kontes and Mankins' book, *The Value Imperative*, which clearly sets out the detail of time value and cash flow calculation.

In simple terms, the following are the main concepts. A company is financed in part by debt and in part by equity. The proportion of the company's capital that is funded by debt is taken at the long-term debt interest rate after deducting the tax effect. The equity portion is taken at the cost of equity capital which can be estimated as follows:

Cost of capital   = risk free rate plus the risk premium

The risk premium = volatility of the   × average risk premium
is taken as   equity cash flow   for the capital market

The volatility factor is generally known as the 'beta' of the business or sector concerned.

While it is not always important for managers to be able to calculate the actual cost of capital in their particular business, they do need to be clear what that cost is. It is also helpful if they are aware of the key assumptions and factors behind that calculation.

Non-financial measures

There are important operational measures and measures of strategic progress that are not financial but they are important. These will differ by industry, perhaps even by geography too. Until recently only scant attention had been paid to finding a way to get effective measurement of strategic progress. Some companies had explicitly included in their strategic plans benchmarks that were measurable and needed to be achieved but they were not incorporated in the reporting systems. One of the key things to remember when designing a reporting system is that it must capture the key measures that will help the management team to monitor progress. The measures that will be monitored will be those that add value and these will often cut across different functions. This is different in emphasis from most systems today that monitor expenses and revenue against budgets that are negotiated annually and are often a compromise!

Perhaps some of the measures companies may include would be objective measures of:

- customer service;
- competitive value for money;
- right-first-time measures;
- time reduction in key business processes;
- innovation and new product development;
- quality;
- supplier performance.

The broad area of non-financial measures is important for two reasons:

1. There are serious limitations to financial measures as they are historical by nature and therefore a poor predictor of the future.
2. They cannot easily reflect the important strategic areas built into plans as a result of a changing environment or changes implemented to pursue a more relevant competitively based strategy.

The keys to success in the future are more likely to include the development and implementation of the right strategy, retaining existing customers through stronger relationships and winning new roles and developing appropriate markets with the right product. All this has to be done cost-effectively which brings attention to the cost of overheads as managers review the business infrastructure.

A good example of a successful manager who thoughtfully addressed the issue of getting the right measures in a business is seen in Case Study 10.2. Bill Hayes of Fabrics Inc. is a real case study but because of the request for anonymity, pseudonyms have been used. It is a good illustration of the fact that non-financial measures are very important and that a company should be measured against strategic goals as well as the more usual financial ones.

Control of overheads

Managers believe implicitly the truism that overheads need to be controlled. This is probably one of the core competences for major companies. Yet it is much more fundamental than simply ensuring that current expenditure is within the allowed budget. Increasingly, managers are reviewing the basic structure that is in place to see if the added value of the different processes is greater than the cost. It is no longer sufficient to make incremental, small savings in overheads because the competition is almost certainly conducting a far-reaching and continuous review of activities to weed out those that do not add value.

Activity-based costing

Many companies are today supplementing traditional approaches to budgetary control and to absorption costing so that they can better understand how costs are really incurred against specified activities. Traditional systems of costing allocate overhead costs rather than focusing on where the costs come from. Activity-based costing (ABC) looks at what are the drivers of those costs. These cost-drivers for activities must be identified. They would include, for example, machine set-up time which is important when variety, as well as machine-running time, is a key issue.

There are a number of consultants and accounting firms which provide services in this area. Their approach follows a common pattern. The first stage is to look at the key business issues facing the corporation and to pull together ways to address these. It is essential to have an external

---
--- **Case Study 10.2** ---

Fabrics Inc. – getting the right measures in a business

Bill Hayes was recently appointed as Managing Director of Fabrics Inc. based in the United Kingdom. The company is a designer and weaver of fabrics in the more fashion forward segment of the market. The historic financial performance of this company was variable and, from a shareholder view, unpredictable. Management had already recognised that on their own they could not compete on costs with cheap sources in Eastern Europe and the Far East and were focusing on quick response and added value. To achieve this, they believed they needed to supplement the traditional and declining customer base with new customers whom they would recruit on the grounds of innovation and design. They would retain the expanded customer base by superior service including fast response to the customers' requirements.

Fabrics Inc. was a traditional company and the accounting and management information systems were quite rudimentary. This was a real frustration for Bill who always felt that he lacked information that would help him to take better decisions. The information available to him could be summarised as:

1. A financial budgeting system.
2. Monthly management accounts.
   - basic variance reports without detail.
3. Half yearly statutory accounts with:
   - an approximate reconciliation to the management accounts;
   - an annual stock check with adjustments taken through the next month's management accounts.
4. A standard costing system which shows gross margins by major product.
5. Other management information which included:
   - the size of the forward order book
   - a monthly factory report which was manually produced showing throughput, efficiency levels and overtime costs.

Bill Hayes wanted his management information system to be linked to the strategy that the company was following and for this information to include appropriate non-financial measures. With his top management team, they listed the deficiencies of the present system then went on to specify what they felt was relevant information for the management of the business.

Frustrations

- No link to strategy or to the future decisions.
- Numbers were historic and where surprises occur there is no answer without a laborious, manual interrogation of the accounts.
- Management did not feel in control but rather were reactive to events.
- No measurement of performance of areas vital to monitor customer requirements.
- The manual system of order/planning/stock was inefficient and not capable of being used for quick response or customer service.

The management team, under Bill Hayes's leadership, decided that they would specify their requirements for information. They started with their mission statement, elucidated the key competitive planks of their strategy and then decided on the critical measurements. In all of this they tried to differentiate themselves from their major competitors.

In summary, their findings were as follows:

Vision. To be the fashion fabric supplier of first choice to the garment industry of Europe thereby achieving market leadership.

Strategic planks

- Outstanding design and reputation for strong innovation.
- Unequalled customer service including the fastest response times to deliver new designs or orders.
- Reduction in cost base to be equal to lowest cost producers in Europe.
- Create higher performance through quality of employees.
- Meet shareholder expectations consistently.

Critical measures

These were divided under the following headings:

Financial	Customer	Other Business Measures
• Cash flow	(a) *Innovation/design*	(b) *Growth*
• Return on capital	• Speed of design to sample (days)	• Per cent sales from new customers
• Earnings per share	• Per cent conversion of new designs to firm orders	• Market share
• Product/ customer segmented profitability	(b) *Service*	(b) *Cost reduction*
	• Days from order to delivery	• Productivity measure
• Working capital per cent to sales	• Per cent orders delivered to time	• Per cent fabric utilisation
• Margins	• Per cent faulty product returned	• Sub-standard production ('damaged and kept')
• Asset turn		• Capacity utilisation including labour
		(c) *Continuous improvement*
		• Investment in training workforce + management
		• Employment practices audit
		• Objective measure of plant and processes *vs* best in the industry.

Bill Hayes and his team gave immediate priority to finding objective ways of developing the following information systems:

1. *Customer service* through an externally conducted annual survey that measured Fabrics Inc. against its competitors through a customer's perspective on the important dimensions of value for money, design, innovation and total service. This gave a customer satisfaction index.

2. *Customer support systems* It was clear that a new computerised order entry system was needed that would enable the company to commit to delivery dates immediately or to respond to enquiries on the status of an order. This system design needed to be integrated to include stock control, factory load planning, raw materials controls and automatic provision of accurate information for monthly accounts. This major system also provided data for a good proportion of the measurements required by the team.

Once the systems had been specified, largely by the management who were very much driving the process, the alternatives were reviewed and a system was chosen with the help of specialist IT services. The system was installed and three years after implementation Bill Hayes observes, 'We now have control of the business by looking at the right measures. Further, the management focus is on issues that make a real difference to our competitiveness and longer-term goals. This is a real change from the fire-fighting approach of the past when we really did not have proper control of the business'.

review. Next, the consultants work with management to define major activities, then follow this by tracking costs to these activities. Each activity will have non-financial characteristics that will need to be described. It is then instructive to match current activities which are undertaken in the company alongside those that are required because they add value and which are highlighted from the external review.

This approach using ABC will often give managers fresh insights which will focus on what drives the costs and how this influences profitability of different products. The analysis also highlights on total non-productive overheads which add no value in the value chain and will usually represent a substantial part of the total.

Once the costs have been identified in this way the ongoing management of the business will change to eliminate as quickly as possible the areas where cost is incurred but no value created. Activities like order-chasing, progressing and correcting past mistakes are all in this category. The study of your business using the methodology of activity-based costing is usually a good initiator of change through business process re-engineering. It is well worthwhile for a manager to look at a pilot study for one part of his business to see what fresh insights he receives and to establish what changes in priority result for the study. For those wishing to understand the detail of ABC and its partner activity-based management a good introduction which is clear and simple to read is found in Cokins, Stratton and Helbling, *An ABC Manager's Primer*. Any manager starting off with an initiative in activity-based costing, they need to be clear at the outset that this requires general management support and endorsement if it is to be taken seriously in the organisation.

Managing value

Finally, an overall view of the business is needed to see if the company is deploying the resources to best effect, delivering genuine shareholder value. We have already seen that traditional accounting measures are an imperfect way of measuring changes in shareholder value. Many companies, no doubt reflecting products from consultants' as well as managements' desire to improve performance, are adopting value-based management techniques. Again, cash flows are key to understanding this approach. In the eyes of the investor, growth only creates value when the cash flow returns in the business exceed investors' requirements. This is useful for segmentation analysis to see which parts of the business are stars in performance and which are the dogs. Clearly, resource allocation will reflect this understanding. However, value-based management can be much more comprehensively applied covering strategic planning to resource allocation, monitoring performance, compensation policy and investor communication. The LEK Partnership is one of the consulting firms that have such a model and Figure 10.4 shows its scheme.

There is another aspect that must not be underplayed and that is the impact of such an approach on the organisation. This is especially true if in addition to taking this approach in measuring performance compensation plans also reflect the same approach. Joel Stern talks about economic value added (EVA) and uses this for long-term incentive plans. He argues that long-term incentive plans should be based on the

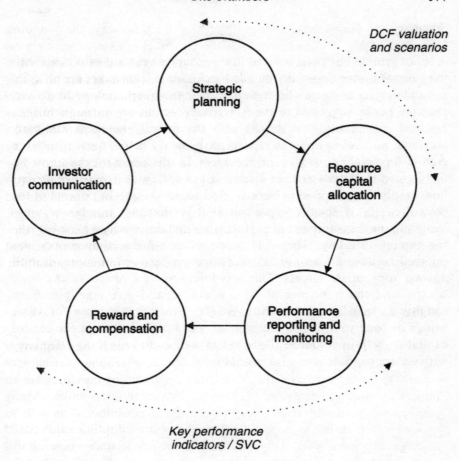

Figure 10.4 Value-based management

value that managers create over and above the cost of capital. If they earn less than the cost of capital they in fact destroy value and should be punished through reducing long-term incentive bonuses by this loss in value.

Value-based management really can influence the culture of the enterprise as managers learn to appreciate the fact that the company must earn at least a return equal to the rate of the cost of capital if they are going to add value. Therefore, marginal capital investments proposed for the company will be measured against this criterion which needs to be well-understood, especially if pay is linked to them.

Summary

A lot of ground has been covered in this chapter yet most of it deals with the general rather than fully detailed techniques. This is appropriate for most managers and any who wish to pursue these topics more deeply can read the books suggested in the References section or pursue them with external consultants. We started with the broadly available company accounts, narrowing down to reports to the board before moving into the area of financial knowledge for managers. In this last-mentioned area we highlighted the importance of discounted cash-flow techniques observing how deeply they are used in business decision-making. The concept of the cost of capital is equally important as it is used in a number of areas including the measurement of performance and decisions on a cut-off rate for capital spending. The wide scope of non-financial measures was pursued because a team, to be motivated properly, must measure itself against appropriate targets. This was followed by a review of overhead control and the principles of ABC which should give managers fresh insights as to where value and costs lie. Finally, managing for value brings us back to a further example of using cash flows and the cost of capital to help in resource allocation as well as in rewarding effectively with an appropriate incentive programme.

11   A Sense of Balance

A successful manager must have the capacity to focus single-mindedly on priorities yet at the same time retain a sense of balance through the recognition of the aspirations and claims of others. This is just one of the great paradoxes of management. To date, in this book, we have focused on some very specific areas that will add value not only to the company but also to the manager through his greater knowledge base. In this chapter we will have regard for a number of areas where a sense of balance is required.

Directors of companies are well aware that their primary objective is to protect shareholders' interests through the maximisation of long-term value for the shareholders. Managers know that to achieve this aim they must have regard for community concerns as well as the aspirations or worries of the workforce. To look at some of these general points in more detail we will examine some important wider issues including corporate governance, balance on the board, cultural diversity and the wider outlook.

Corporate governance

The Cadbury Report in the United Kingdom is a landmark establishing minimum standards in accounting and in annual reporting. The timing of this was perfect because it was tabled when there was a groundswell of concern on wider aspects of corporate governance. Some of this concern was rooted in a floodtide of worldwide corporate failures, often unexpected, when large chunks of shareholder value were destroyed. What seemed to be worst of all was that managers and directors appeared to act inappropriately, even fraudulently in some cases. In this environment many people questioned the market enterprise system which is the backbone of Western economies. Classical eighteenth-century economists proclaimed that consumers and producers striving to achieve their own selfish aims would enhance economic welfare for the whole society. However, in today's world of fierce competition and fairly short-term requirements of investors it was agreed that business ethics suffered if there was no room to incur non-essential costs. After all, we have already observed that the primary function of a company is to maximise profits within the framework of the law.

Yet this is too simple a concept. It does not reflect the judgements that managers need to make. It reminds me of the saying, 'man needs to eat to live'. Yet life is much more than eating, just as managing is much more than maximising profits. Companies can pursue profits while maintaining proper ethical standards, reflecting good corporate governance in all that they do. There is no doubt that such well-run companies recognised for their high ethical standards, are positively received in the communities in which they operate. A positive community supporting the enterprise is a real asset both in the good times as well as those that are not. Recruiting the best people is easier in a successful, ethical company.

The Cadbury Report laid down a code of best practice which is summarised in Figure 11.1. It also made some very important observations and recommendations. The main recommendations of the Cadbury Report have been taken up by most major companies in the United Kingdom and have been examined around the world. The board of directors is asked to consider those items which it reserves for itself so that all directors and managers are clear about where the authority lies. There needs to be balance on the board. This requires a sufficient number of independent non-executive directors who are sufficiently well-informed to act as 'devil's advocate' and to bring good, balanced judgement from their wider perspective. Importantly, but initially controversially, there should be separation of the roles of chairman and chief executive although it was recognised that exceptions to this rule could be possible. If the roles, for good reason, were not separated then a leader of non-executives was suggested as a way to bring balance. A further area which caused great debate was the Cadbury suggestion that the role of non-executive directors should encompass monitoring management including the executive directors whose contracts of employment should not be longer than three years. Many commentators observed that this 'policeman role' for non-executives would be divisive, especially as under company law all directors have equal responsibilities.

Companies were also encouraged to continue with the concept of balance through the setting up of specific board committees staffed mainly by non-executive directors. These included nomination committees to provide specialist, detailed oversight on the accounts, directors' remuneration and appointments of new directors respectively.

Companies are required to report on the extent to which they comply with the Cadbury Code and the directors' statement on this matter is subject to audit. This is now a requirement for companies to retain their listing on the stock market.

Figure 11.1

The code of best practice formulated by the committee on the financial aspects of corporate governance ('the Cadbury Code')

1. The Board of Directors

1.1 The Board should meet regularly, retain full and effective control over the company and monitor the Executive Management.

1.2 There should be a clearly accepted division of responsibilities at the head of a company, which will ensure a balance of power and authority, such that no one individual has unfettered powers of decision. Where the Chairman is also the Chief Executive, it is essential that there should be a strong and independent element on the Board, with a recognised senior member.

1.3 The Board should include non-Executive Directors of sufficient calibre and number for their views to carry significant weight in the Board's decisions.

1.4 The Board should have a formal schedule of matters specifically reserved to it for decision to ensure that the direction and control of the company is firmly in its hands.

1.5 There should be an agreed procedure for Directors in the furtherance of their duties to take independent professional advice if necessary, at the company's expense.

1.6 All directors should have access to the advice and services of the Company Secretary, who is responsible to the Board for ensuring that Board procedures are followed and that applicable rules and regulations are complied with. Any question of the removal of the Company Secretary should be a matter for the Board as a whole.

2. Non-Executive Directors

2.1 Non-Executive Directors should bring an independent judgement to bear on issues of strategy, performance, resources, including key appointments, and standards of conduct.

2.2 The majority should be independent of management and free from any business or other relationship which could materially interfere with the exercise of their independent judgement,

Figure 11.1 continued overleaf

---

apart from their fees and shareholding. Their fee should reflect the time which they commit to the company.

2.3 Non-Executive Directors should be appointed for specified terms and re-appointment should not be automatic.

2.4 Non-Executive Directors should be selected through a formal process and both this process and their appointment should be a matter for the Board as a whole.

3.   Executive Directors

3.1 Directors' service contracts should not exceed three years without shareholders' approval.

3.2 There should be full and clear disclosure of Directors' total emoluments and those of the Chairman and highest paid UK Director, including pension contributions and stock options. Separate figures should be given for salary and performance related elements and the basis on which performance is measured should be explained.

3.3 Executive Directors' pay should be subject to the recommendations of a Remuneration Committee made up wholly or mainly of non-Executive Directors.

4.   Reporting and Controls

4.1 It is the Board's duty to present a balanced and understandable assessment of their company's position.

4.2 The Board should ensure that an objective and professional relationship is maintained with the Auditors.

4.3 The Board should establish an Audit Committee of at least three non-Executive Directors with written terms of reference which deal clearly with its authority and duties.

4.4 The Directors should explain their responsibility for preparing the financial statements next to a statement by the Auditors about their reporting responsibilities.

4.5 The Directors should report on the effectiveness of the company's system of Internal Control.

4.6 The Directors should report that the business is a going concern, with supporting assumptions or qualifications as necessary.

Figure 11.1 'The Cadbury Code'

The best-run companies will not only adhere to the Cadbury Committee Code of best practice but will also have in place a 'Statement of Values' which will capture the ethos of the company. A typical statement of values is shown in Figure 11.2. Words by themselves are empty, they need to be lived day by day. Managers need to be sure that the spirit of Cadbury, and the balance it requires, are seen in the living example of their actions.

A question of reward

The British press has, in recent times, been keenly interested in executive salaries, especially those of directors of public companies. It is always good knock-about stuff to expose high payments to a handful of people in a community! The interest of the press and the public at large has been aroused because of a combination of three things:

1. Some remuneration packages look difficult to justify from the external comparisons of peer-group payments or from the performance of the particular company.
2. Failed executive directors removed from office have typically received substantial payoffs for failure, reflecting the tenure of their contracts which would usually be three years rolling.
3. The recently privatised utilities have taken the opportunity of increasing salaries and rewards substantially to reflect the going rate for similar-sized companies.

In a number of cases the timing has been insensitive and the arguments supporting the increases have been less than convincing.

All this is happening at a time of heightened awareness of corporate governance so that there is an easy label on which to place a general attack on rewards. Within a worldwide context, it would seem peculiarly British that high financial rewards are applauded in the field of pop music, entertainment and sport, yet are regarded as distastefully inappropriate in business. Interestingly, professional service providers, whether in finance, law, consultancy or banking, are exempt from this criticism. It would, however, be wrong to assume that the current controversy is simply because of the media's approach in presenting a largely negative picture. Politicians talk on one side of the House of 'the undeserving rich' while on the other side the Opposition are accused of

If management decisions are to be delegated as closely as possible to the point of greatest impact, the group must have shared values which guide decision-making. The following eight points are statements of value for our group.

1. **Competitive ability**

   We must be competitive in the market place, today and tomorrow, maintaining our products' edge and identify against the competition. We compete on quality, service and value. This means innovating, analysing, taking risks and making decisions consistent with our values.

2. **Quality, service and value**

   The key characteristics we must aim for in every respect of the group's activities are quality, service and value. Our products sell on this premise and the best way to cement partnerships with customers is by adding value in this way. We need to deliver value for money through manufacturing excellence coupled with appropriate commercially focused research. Our policy is to focus on quality in all that we do: quality products for our consumers, and quality service to our customers.

3. **Taking advantage of change**

   Change is constant in markets, in ideas, in people, and in technology. We therefore need to have decisive leadership and fast management reaction to secure maximum advantage from such changes.

4. **Committed people**

   Committed people are key to our group's success. People must know what is required of them and should be given help to meet those expectations. Our standards should be demanding and this will require appropriate rewards. We are fully committed to equality of opportunity in all aspects of employment and appointments are made solely on the basis of an individual's ability to meet job requirements. The employment of individuals with diverse cultural backgrounds is openly encouraged as a value to the organisation.

5. **Clear objectives**

Our group must have clarity of purpose to compete effectively. Its strategy must be clearly communicated and the objectives which flow from the strategy, both corporate and individual, must be understood. Objectives must be attainable and their achievement should stretch the abilities of those for whom they are set. Managers must build their competences to improve their changes of complete success. Each manager will be held accountable for the attainment of his or her objectives.

6. **Simple organisation**

We must concentrate on the key tasks of the business and all decisions should be taken as close as possible to the point of impact. The organisation should reflect the market and customer focus of the business, with as few layers as possible.

7. **Openness**

An openness of style and involvement of people in the decisions that affect them is of the greatest importance. It requires of management trust and an ability to weigh up and decide.

8. **Responsibilities**

Our group recognises its responsibilities to all shareholders, employees, customers, suppliers, governments and society. It will seek to keep its responsibilities to them in balance.

Figure 11.2 Statement of values

promoting 'the politics of envy'. However, there are real concerns being raised by the public at large that need to be addressed. These include:

- the size and shape of the remuneration packages;
- the contractual tenure of senior employees;
- transparency of procedures and awards.

Role of reward packages

To provide a degree of balance to the discussion, it is helpful to set down the role of reward packages, understanding how these are shaped in the best long-term interests of shareholders. Any remuneration policy will need to ensure that it is capable of:

- Recruiting the best talent;
- Retaining key executives who are performing;
- Motivating management to be over-achievers and focused on agreed goals.

In addition, reward packages must be supportive of the business objectives so that there is compatibility rather than conflict.

The menu of benefits can be summarised under the following headings:

- salary and perks;
- deferred income, for example, payments made into a pension scheme;
- short-term (usually annual) bonuses tailored to meet performance against agreed targets or objectives
- profit-sharing where a pool of profits is divided on an agreed basis amongst management;
- a long-term incentive plan, typically over three years or perhaps five years based on comparative long-term growth;
- share options which need to be held for three to ten years;
- deferred income, for example, payments made into a pension scheme.

The selection of the appropriate group of rewards requires judgement on the part of the decision maker to include those elements that have the best fit between meeting the criteria of recruiting, retaining and motivating but which also meet the corporate objectives. There will therefore be an appropriate variety of packages in different companies reflecting different needs at any point of time.

Remuneration committee

Almost all British companies comply with the Cadbury recommendations and have a remuneration committee made up of non-executive directors, one of whom is chairman. Their role is to ensure that the reward package is appropriate, specifically to examine top salaries and rewards and, annually, to agree changes. The best remuneration committees have a strong, independent chairman who is well-informed with separate advice on general as well as specific remuneration issues. The chairman is encouraged to take separate advice to test any recommendations that are, of necessity, internally generated.

Those who would detract from the specific Cadbury Committee recommendation on remuneration suggest that independence is not perfect when directors are in fact colleagues on the same board. Some elements of the press have been more colourful in their questioning, suggesting that there is a conspiracy of overpaying. The idea put forward is that 'all have their snouts in the same feedbox'. This is a disingenuous argument which goes directly to the integrity and professionalism of non-executive directors. There would be less than a handful of truly professional non-executive directors who would allow themselves to be compromised in this way. Certainly, they would not allow the relatively modest payments from directors' fees to influence their judgement or integrity!!

Way forward

There is an issue of public concern that must be addressed and which cannot be swept under the carpet. The public at large must see the remuneration committee as independent, professional and staffed with members who have integrity and judgement. Part of the answer is in the choice of people on the committee while the other part is found in the transparency of decision-making and the ability to communicate effectively to the appropriate audience. The annual report should include full details of the basis of remuneration decisions, especially in the case of performance bonuses. Best practice requires that each director's salary, perks, bonuses and pension contributions as well as the potential or actual benefits from share options be separately shown.

Given this openness and rational explanation, the heat should be removed from the debate and any ill-informed comments seen for what they are. The remaining issue is the question of tenure of contracts of employment. In today's environment, my view is that a two-year initial contract which reverts to one year rolling, should normally be the longest contractual time for the most senior executives. This would reduce potential payments for non-performance to reasonable levels. In my view, highly performing executives should be very well paid, while those who do not perform should be quite quickly removed.

The current climate of generic criticism of high payments and open attack on business executives by segments of the population is likely to damage the confidence and performance of good managers. It is wasteful of scarce time for senior executives to be dealing with negative, ill-informed comments. They can spend their time more effectively building shareholder value. Inevitably, mobile managers will vote with their feet moving internationally if they do not feel valued.

Balance on the board

There are high expectations of the board of directors. I fear that in many respects these expectations are unrealistic. This follows as the community have a variety of views about the role of the board. This has already been touched on in Chapter 7 as well as earlier in this chapter with the discussion of the Cadbury Report. The aspect that is the focus here is one of great interest for general managers, especially if they are also directors of the company.

It will be clear to all newly appointed directors, executive or non-executive, that they have obligations in law. The executive directors may find themselves serving on a board where their boss, as chief executive, is a member alongside several other senior executives. The balance that needs to be struck is the broader contribution which is required at board meetings without other colleagues feeling that an element of cleverness has crept in for personal reasons. For me it is easy. The chief executive should create the climate where any of his direct reports who are also colleagues as company directors can contribute openly and freely at board meetings. As a matter of good practice as well as courtesy, if a controversial view is likely on an item well-signalled on the agenda, the executive should take the initiative to discuss his views in advance with executive directors affected. This will always include the chief executive, probably the finance director and, if another division is involved, then certainly the head of that division.

Openness

Perhaps the worst situation of all exists when directors do not feel able to express a contrary view in case the solidarity of executive directors is broken down. The Demb and Neubauer European Research Project in corporate governance reflects on a number of failures where the board made bad decisions. There are examples from their work that illustrate that in a boardroom atmosphere that is not truly open it is very difficult for non- executives to press home areas that might be controversial or where the wider experience might bring better judgement. In one case which they quote, the board was unaware that a project put forward for substantial investment in USA was only put forward by the American management of this English-based public company because the Americans believed that this plant was required by the corporate centre for wider strategic reasons. In fact, the United Kingdom business had already invested about £25m in a product-specific plant which was successful and for which product the company had worldwide aspirations. The market research in USA indicated that the successful United Kingdom product would only be a niche player within the different market of the USA, and would be largely unprofitable. Their analysis concluded that purely from an American market viewpoint the investment was not justified. However, the centre pressed hard to ensure it was not just a case of 'not invented here' which was interpreted by the Americans as a need to support this worldwide initiative.

There was no discussion of this at the board. The carefully couched language of the American presenter drew heavily on the UK success, the need for more capacity even though per capita sales in USA were likely to be much lower. This lack of openness was costly as the American plant was never used beyond about 20 per cent of its capacity because the product failed in the market test area. The plant was cannibalised for other production.

Good, open relations between the board and the chief executive are also required if this is to be a productive partnership. Trust needs to be built up through excellent communication and appropriate early involvement of the board on important or sensitive matters. This requires a constant dialogue with the board so that the 'no surprises' rule is always effectively pursued. The chief executive and the chairman will have agreed between themselves and explicitly with the board how their separate roles will work in practice. A lot of work is required to maintain the essential good relations between the two at the top.

The chief executive should always ensure that there is direct contact with each non-executive at appropriate times and with the chairman and non-executives separately. Opportunities for deeper learning by non-executive directors around business reviews, budgets and especially strategic plans are very important. Their wider input is invaluable to a chief executive who will occasionally and quite freely talk to individual non-executives on specific issues where they have special expertise or experience.

Exposing yourself

Employees in an organisation really appreciate a spirit of openness where they feel that there is no hidden agenda on big issues. They would feel that this climate provides fertile grounds for contributing more freely to the company's progress through being more involved. As far as managers are concerned, those who are open in their relationships and communications are typically more confident in their role. They will be comfortable with sharing information reasonably early in the scheme of things, knowing that they may well need to change things on the margins according to the differing conditions encountered.

As Chief Executive, I have indicated in the past that 'a leader must be comfortable exposing oneself'. This means that in external or internal communication, a confident leader will indicate hopes, aspirations and objectives knowing full well that on a number of occasions the situation will change. For example, a non-core subsidiary may be put up for sale after a clear external evaluation indicates that there are potential buyers and the likely price will be acceptable to the vendor. However, as the process unfolds, it may become clear that the sale cannot be effected at a price that adds value to the vendor's shareholders. Where the value gap is significant the management will need to abort the sale and continue to manage the company in the now difficult environment of uncertainty and explain credibly why this course is taken.

There are many managers who take a different approach, communicating nothing until the last moment, to avoid any 'embarrassing climbdown'. While this might appear a safer route for managers, the trade-off is a loss of credibility with the internal and external audience. The company becomes one known as secretive or surprising.

Yet, even with the concept of openness there is a need for balance. First, the troops within will be confused if the messages are constantly changed and communication indicates that different directions are being followed at frequent intervals. There is also a case to be made that would, on the margins, limit the amount of communication to avoid giving out competitively useful information. This argument is usually overstated as in practice the information cannot readily be utilised by the competition. However, the issue is one that needs to be watched, especially when the corporate magazine is used to inform staff about a new product or process. This is usually the most indiscrete area and there is no doubt that the staff magazine of one company will be avidly read by all its competitors, major customers and suppliers.

I have been accused occasionally of being open to the point of indiscretion. While I would like to think this is a harsh judgement and an overstatement, there is certainly an element of truth in this. Therefore, while I remain a very strong advocate of openness in any organisation, to get issues out early in the process I need to remember about balance to avoid the downsides that are obvious where openness is practised to the extreme.

Cultural diversity

Chances are that managers thinking about cultural diversity and its relevance to the world of business will think first of equal opportunities legislation. Talking with managers on the topic will usually elicit a defensive posture coupled with examples of their good corporate citizenship. When pressed further, they will typically argue that they have made excellent progress in delivering their commitment to equal opportunities. Often, the management of the better companies will point to their public 'values statement' to make the point.

At Esso they state:

'the company will recruit, develop and treat its employees on the basis of their relevant skills, aptitudes and abilities. The criteria for making these decisions will be those determined only by the performance and ability of the individual and the requirements of available jobs. It is the company's aim to ensure that no applicant or employee receives less favourable treatment on the grounds of race, colour, sex, marital status, religion, ethics or national origin.'

The Esso statement goes on at some length covering the implementation of this policy alongside harassment in the workplace and procedures that apply in the event of this problem.

Other companies will tend to be less prescriptive relying more on broad principles and the spirit of equal opportunities. Something along the following minimum statement, backed up with genuine commitment, is the alternative. 'This company is fully committed to equality of opportunity in all aspects of employment and appointments are made on the basis of an individual's ability to meet job requirements. The employment of individuals with diverse cultural backgrounds is openly encouraged as a major plank of employment policy'.

Statements like these are laudable. They need to be lived out in everyday life at the enterprise. Most managers to whom I have spoken on this subject will agree the concept readily enough, talk about progress to date and openly admit that there is much more to do. They will observe only a small proportion of women senior managers or of ethnic minorities then highlight the efforts being made to directionally change this. Pressure groups have seen their role as increasing the total stock of minorities in much the same way as accumulating points at a sporting event.

Advantage in diversity

There is no doubt that overall progress is being made with social justice in the workforce and this should be applauded. However, it is not anywhere near real progress for the company that wants to deliver competitive advantage from its workforce. As we enter the next millennium the companies that can celebrate the benefits of diversity as a very positive and necessary initiative will be competitive winners. This is, first, because the company will enhance the quality of its decision-making with the rich differing experiences from a kaleidoscope of backgrounds of its employees. Second, the company will attract the best people who see clearly that it is a meritocracy where everyone feels valued and their talents are fully utilised.

Diversity is an amalgam of visible and non-visible differences which can be utilised to create a more productive environment where talent is recognised in its own right. This is quite different from 'equal opportunities' which is often seen as being about ethnic minorities, the role of women, disabled people or sexual preferences. Many companies today are really discovering how to make diversity pay. This is the positive side of diversity which is central to the message in this section. Increasingly, companies are becoming international in outlook or by direct involvement because of the impact of internationalism that affects us all.

There is an advantage for the international company that is able to build the skills that enable it to work harmoniously and productively in many different countries each with a different dimension of culture. For a company to outperform its competition there is a need to establish and develop the core competence of empathy and understanding in these very different circumstances. It is an asset to be able to recognise difference in cultures and to use this understanding to further the corporation's goals.

Where alliances or joint ventures are chosen to execute the strategy, then a deep understanding of different styles is essential. This not only avoids misunderstanding but provides a platform to build trust, to overcome frictions that will inevitably arise. As an example, in 1993 a group of fourteen Toshiba and Siemens engineers had been working with IBM at their technology centre to develop a twenty-first century 25-million-bit chip. The group had some interesting learning experiences on different styles of working which were reported in the Siemens review.

While there have been a number of academic studies that have concluded that diversity can enhance performance, the practical manager would rather see examples from the real world.

An example of wholehearted support for people of diverse backgrounds contributing real value comes from Hoechst Celanese the chemical giant. Ernest H. Drew, the CEO, is a public enthusiast of the concept that diversity pays. He describes cultural diversity in his company's workforce as a 'silver lining' and that management performance has been significantly enhanced because of a diverse management group. They have also set bold goals for the beginning of the twenty-first century. Throughout the organisation of Hoechst Celanese, Drew wants to see 34 per cent representation through all levels of management of women and minorities. This 34 per cent target exactly mirrors the company's projected workforce.

If managers want diversity to be a strong, positive benefit in their company they need to accept that hard work will be needed to tap into this asset. There will be setbacks to overcome, some disappointments as well as a joyful celebration of the successes. The top management must be committed to the programme including the training, coaching and mentoring of all components of the management group and workforce.

Still, those managers who crack this nut will find pleasure in their new environment as well as competitive advantage by tapping this rich vein of potential.

There are, of course, plenty of difficulties in managing across differing cultures. It requires patience and understanding in addition to the investment of time, to see nationals at work in their own country. In Case Study 11.1 there is a summary of a Case Study set in China. In this example things did not work out too well, resulting in some important lessons being learned.

The wider outlook

Managers today are hard-pressed because of the span of their work following the removal of layers in the organisation. They are buffeted by the constant change which is a feature of their environment and the need for speedy decisions. Single-minded pursuit of objectives is called for by the company to a degree that was unheard of even 10 or 15 years ago. There is a need for strong, emotional resilience to cope with this world. Yet, more than this, successful managers recognise that they are part of a community even when they know that their term of office in the particular area is finite.

─────────── **Case Study 11.1** ───────────

Aspects of cultural diversity

Omega is a fictitious company used to illustrate a real-life experience of a UK-based company in manufacturing products sold to industrial customers for use in production of consumer products. Omega has a presence in all the major regions of the world but only has a very small presence in China. However, it does have a respectable business in Hong Kong where it has been manufacturing for some years. It also has a presence in Taiwan and over the past 10 years has built up this presence through the efforts of Chang, a Hong Kong Chinese who has built up a team of good Chinese managers. Financial performance has been satisfactory, yet unspectacular, and the company was becoming increasingly worried about the transfer of their customers' business to mainland China. To date, the only presence in China was a sales office in Guangzhou and Shanghai staffed by expatriate Hong Kong Chinese managers.

Chang was an impressive man with excellent contacts in Hong Kong and also in a number of provinces in China. He was an opportunist who saw many opportunities to create value. He would set up small units to attack a niche market, sometimes with a 'front man' who would be a partner in a limited joint venture. His management team were fiercely loyal to him, and through him to the company. Group management of Omega were delighted to have someone like Chang to lead the team who was clearly so well-tuned to the local people and to local opportunities. They recognised that Chang was less than perfect in his communication upwards and were sometimes surprised by actions taken which would normally require prior approval.

Chang, over the past two years, spent most of his direct contact time with the head office talking in general, perhaps vague terms, about the grand vision of 'Son of Omega' in China involving a complete replication of manufacturing plant covering all four of the complex sequential manufacturing processes. He also spoke of the need to have a strong local partner and he would talk enthusiastically about those thought to be best and who were well-known to Chang.

Group management listened attentively, feeling intuitively that a strategic move into China was appropriate and would in fact be an imperative in the next five years. However, they were frustrated with the absence of facts supporting the proposal which doggedly remained couched in general terms. They were concerned about the complexity and could not understand why Chang was adamant over the need for all four stages of the manufacturing process. It would be a very large undertaking requiring technical and financial support of a large order. Chang was clear that he would be able to find local Chinese talent that could be trained initially by a battery of expatriates. He also made it clear that as an entrepreneur he would like a personal stake in the new Chinese venture.

Group management asked for a full evaluation and report on the way forward which Chang promised would be fully documented and would be completed in three months. When the document arrived there was a feeling of disbelief from group management who felt that the proposal was vague, unstructured and lacking in any hard financial evaluation. They therefore seconded a group accountant to put it into shape for the normal capital approval process. Chang was disappointed and insisted that this was a strategic move which could not be properly evaluated in this way. The financial evaluation prepared by the group accountant demonstrated that there certainly was no financial case as the internal rate of return was less than half the cost of capital of Omega and the payback in cash terms would be more than 10 years.

The main board asked Chang to reconsider the proposal fundamentally as they rejected his submission. Chang resigned because he had lost face with his team who saw promotional prospects and because his potential partners believed that the entry strategy into China involving them was as good as a 'done deal'. Nearly two-thirds of the top Chinese team resigned with Chang as they felt primary allegiance to him. This severely set back Omega in Hong Kong where they had to send in a team of UK expatriates to try to rebuild the management. Omega is still trying to recover the position and has put any idea of entry into China on to a very distant back-burner.

Key Lessons

1. Group management did not understand the culture of the Chinese team or their indirect and general way of dealing with a big issue.
2. Group management failed to appropriately monitor and control their activities in Hong Kong by largely abdicating management to the local team which was loyal to Chang first.
3. Group management were unrealistic in assuming that because the Chinese senior team spoke good English that they thought and acted like them.

Community involvement

Wise companies encourage community involvement, not only for the positive impact of good community relations, but, frankly, because the community as a stakeholder needs input from managers to help effectiveness in the various areas of endeavour. There are many examples of involvement with schools, local councils, local charities or sports clubs where managers give their time and where companies lend their support. The charitable donations policy of many companies today reflects community support by matching funds raised by staff for local activities or to support local managers giving their time.

Managers will also need to be aware of or integrated into local politics through key figures of associations as well as supporting, where possible, effective trade or industry bodies. Of course, the level of management is a factor in determining the time devoted to these areas but it remains essential for managers to have a wide range of influences. Many managers also find it valuable to know at first hand their opposite numbers in the main competitors. This does not propose a cosy relationship but it does provide the opportunity to talk through potential misunderstandings. The astute manager will also learn about the application of his competitor's strategy through such interchanges; a fact which should not be forgotten in reverse!

Non-executive experience

There is another enriching experience that provides breadth of knowledge, which is potentially available to many managers. The role of the non-executive director is one that is being emphasised in the current environment of increased corporate responsibility. Many companies will recognise the two-way benefits of having senior managers participate as non-executive directors in a non-competing company where there are no conflicts to manage. Usually the more enlightened companies will allow managers to accept one such appointment, recognising that while this requires an investment of time, the responsible manager will balance his time amongst his priorities so that the main job does not in any way suffer.

The manager is able to learn from this different experience utilising concepts that may have common application, and learning the technique of pursuing the big issues. Self-confidence is bolstered when the new non-executive director finds that he/she can quickly grasp the fundamentals in a new business, and make a balanced effective contribution to a different board of directors.

Summary

A sense of balance is very much needed by the manager who would be successful. In this chapter we have looked at some areas where a wider view helps the quality of decision-making by the successful manager. Additionally, we have identified the potential added value both to the company and the individual through applying best practice in corporate governance. This is important to a manager who needs to establish a high reputation for competence and high principles. A manager's greatest asset is his/her integrity and reputation. If this goes, no matter how talented, how remarkable his/her track record, the manager is ineffective. While for some managers the question of balance of the board may seem a subject that can be left until a little later in their career, there are insights that will help their development today. They will also be more effective in their current role if they recognise and act today with understanding of the issues.

When we dwell on cultural diversity we awaken an awareness that this issue is not about compliance. There are rich seams of gold to be mined by taking this concept and making it work positively for the company. A sense of balance is a key prerequisite for a successful manager.

12   A Distillation

Value creation

The central proposition that runs through this book is that managers are employed to create shareholder value. This is their prime aim, their central focus in making the choice of emphasis from their individual list of priorities. They need to identify from their own area of influence those items that really do add value at the end of the process, and those that do not. The starting-point is that any non-value adding activities identified should be scrapped. This action should not be taken in isolation or without appropriate discussion to ensure that the full implications from the total business chain are taken into account. Managers will not win bouquets for creating problems elsewhere in the value chain by abandoning activities they can personally avoid, only to pass on problems elsewhere in the business. This is why a holistic approach is needed.

Lessons from successful companies give a clear lead to managers that winners focus on those things that are truly important, while losers spray in a random way. Therefore, successful managers will ensure that their annual objectives fully reflect the priorities in accordance with the value-creating opportunities that are available in their current role. They will find occasions for networking both within the firm as well as outside, utilising every opportunity to find new ways of improving their performances.

To outperform their peers in this competitive arena, managers who have an outward curiosity and a wide range of interests are more likely to find fresh, creative ways of adding value.

Whatever role managers face they are likely to be supplicants for resources, especially finance for capital projects. The production manager, for example, will always have an eye on the latest techniques and new items of plant that add flexibility or productivity. The drive to reduce manufacturing costs or add product flexibility at no additional cost is a potent driver of demand for capital. Experience shows that production managers who understand the commercial imperatives of a business are more likely to put forward a compelling case for capital expenditure. This requires a knowledge of discounted cash flow techniques and a thorough understanding of their own company's financial criteria. In particular, the manager should have a good understanding of the cost of capital for the business, for no rational decision-maker will approve a capital expenditure that delivers a return of less than that capital over the life of the project. These important points are covered more fully in Chapter 10. To illustrate the scope of financial objectives, Figure 12.1 lists the actual financial criteria for a conglomerate company in the United Kingdom.

1. The primary aim of the business is to generate an operational cash flow (OCF) to sales of more than 8 per cent. (Note: OCF is trading profit (i.e. before interest, taxes and dividend) plus depreciation and other non-cash items.)
2. Group earnings per share growth of 7 per cent plus inflation in the long term.
3. The return on capital employed (ROCE) should be not less than 20 per cent. (ROCE is trading profit divided by the average capital employed, excluding investments.)
4. Interest cover should be greater than five times (i.e. the number of times interest payments are covered by trading profits).
5. Gearing should be less than 40 per cent based on the end-of-year balance sheet, in the longer term. Temporary gearing of up to 60 per cent is acceptable provided that interest cover is maintained. (Gearing is calculated as total debt divided by total equity.)
6. Dividends should increase at least in line with inflation. The objective dividend cover is two times. When the objective dividend cover is reached, dividends will increase in line with earnings. (Dividend cover is tax-paid profits divided by total dividends paid.)

Figure 12.1 Company XYZ Plc: financial criteria

Core themes

There have been four core themes that have run through this book. These are the central messages that have come through from the specific topics covered by each of the chapters. For this, the distillation of what has already been written, we will dip into the topics already covered to rearrange some of the fundamental points into the four core themes. As a reminder, the four themes are:

1. Change is continuous.
2. Strategy is fundamental.
3. There is a real dependence on people.
4. Leadership is key.

We will review each of these in turn.

1. Change is continuous

We have recognised the inescapable truth that change is all around us, is fast-moving and accelerating, and is permanent. There is no escaping this and managers must be comfortable within this arena. While economists still search for conditions of equilibrium at the firm within its competitive setting, this is an increasingly rare event. Today, equilibrium of the firm is about as frequent as an eclipse of the sun.

There are some clear implications for managers from this observation of continuous change.

First, they must develop the ability to think clearly about the issues impacting on each particular area requiring decision, and must be prepared to make trade-offs, to optimise, and arrive at speedy decisions. There is no room for analysing to death or, on the other hand, for sloppy thinking. Depending upon the impact of the decision on the business, appropriate analysis must be done, an early decision taken and adjustments made on the move as more facts or experience are gained. It is much better to make an early decision that is 80 per cent correct and make the final adjustments during implementation than to analyse to the last decimal point of a non-critical factor. Remember the concept of 'ready, fire, aim'!

Second, in a fast-changing world where businesses and managers are buffeted around by external forces, managers need to be nimble, to respond capably to keep the company on track and to meet its objectives. This implies an organisation that is empowered to make decisions as close as possible to the point of impact. Managers and the workforce must be appropriately prepared for this by way of both training and communication. It also follows that successful managers will have developed appropriate interpersonal and communication skills.

Third, managers will need to be increasingly outwardly focused, aware of important trends that may impact on their work space and the life space of their industry and company. This means wide reading, exercising curiosity and the hardest part of all, thinking about the implications. It does not mean forecasting a scenario of dubious probability, rather it means thinking about important trends and how they may impact.

Fourth, on the personal front, given these pressures, given flatter organisations and greater work responsibility, emotional resilience is an essential element in a successful manager. All managers need to be able to cope with the pressures on them. There are recognised ways to help to achieve this even for managers who find stress more difficult to deal with. Perhaps the most important thing of all is to find balance in our lives creating space for work, for family, for outside interests including physical and spiritual areas.

2. Strategy is fundamental

Chapter 6 deals specifically with strategy. The key proposition is made that, even in a fast-changing world, there is a great benefit in having a clear goal and a plan of how to get there. The plan is not written in stone, for successful managers know that there will be plenty of occasions when the business will be blown off course. New competitors will arrive or old ones will suddenly and without warning take an action designed to weaken the business. Managers will react to continue towards the goal, perhaps making a deviation or two on the way. Knowing where you are going and communicating that through an organisation is a powerful enabler to gain superior performance for the shareholders.

As companies and their products become more influenced by global factors and as more alliances add to complexity, a good strategic plan is essential. It must be based on quality analysis rather than wishful thinking yielding a sustainable competitive advantage that is truly based on a firm foundation of competences within the firm. The exercise is hard work, demanding rigour and quality thinking but within a company it builds teams that are motivated to deliver to the standards set down.

Finally, communication of the strategy in a layered way is an essential part of the process. At board level, the strategy must be clearly understood in sufficient detail so that the board can agree appropriation of resources and can measure the business objectively. As you go down through the organisation, the top-level strategy should be more general and the individual areas should be more specific.

Strategy is a fundamentally important way of addressing value and is a significant factor in the long-term superior performance of successful companies.

3. *Dependence on people*

Why is it, when almost every manager knows that committed, talented people are so essential for superior performance, that this aspect of management still receives insufficient attention? We saw in the survey that both personal development and management development received 4 per cent and 8 per cent of their time respectively. Given the crucial importance of these roles this is not enough. We all need to do better.

No matter how good the company's management development plan, a manager cannot rely on this for his/her future. Younger managers especially must realise that they are responsible for preparing and implementing their personal development plan, and discussing it with a superior or mentor, if this is applicable. Realism is important, just as is the value of a varied career in differing learning situations.

Winning companies in the future will have built a competitive advantage from the skill, energy and commitment of their people. This includes all levels of management but, importantly, should also embrace the workforce who can contribute so much. There are clear implications of this which successful managers will pick up.

First, training programmes will need to reflect more accurately the future needs distilled from an evaluation of future trends in the environment. This requires analysis as well as thoughtfulness and then single-minded determination to implement these plans. Unfortunately, in financially stressful times, training budgets are easily plundered to help to rescue short-run profit needs. The problem is that this vicious circle ensnares the manager continuously and the step-change in capability is never achieved.

Second, we have noted that management development succession plans and training programmes need a higher priority. Perhaps the first step is to include measurable benchmarks in this area as key objectives for each executive. This could be coupled with awarding part of the annual bonus according to achievement of this very important personal goal. Management incentive programmes are a good way of rewarding appropriate behaviour and changing the culture of an organisation.

Third, we should all recognise that if we spent a little more time of our own personal development, planning it, developing new skills and investing time in it, this example is likely to rub off on our peers as well as those who report to us. Check how much time you spend on your personal development against the meagre 4 per cent average for our sample of senior successful managers.

4. Leadership

All of us would like to be seen as good leaders. The concept can be seen as one of power with all the responsibility that this brings. It is an essential element of any successful manager yet it remains incredibly difficult to define. Part of the problem is that when we think of a great leader we tend to think of a powerful, often charismatic, person. This is all too limiting in dealing with leadership in the business setting. In Chapter 2 there are illustrations that should help towards understanding the scope of leadership as well as evidence that leadership skills can and must be developed or learnt.

In Figure 12.2, 'Key Messages for Managers', under key point 5, there are ten descriptions that try to give a picture of the essence of successful leadership. A great leader has a vision of where he would like to take his followers which is clearly communicated. Clear expectations are set at each level in the organisation that are based on realistic, understandable strategies. Then the capability of the people must be developed so that in the end the management team can say 'see what we have done together to transform this business'.

Figure 12.2

Underlying message

- Managers must focus on how they can use their efforts to maximise shareholder value.
- Every manager should focus on the unique contribution to value that he or she can bring.
- Any business that earns less than the cost of capital on its investments is destroying shareholder value.

Key points

1. Those wishing to promote managers either internally or externally look at the track record for evidence of:

   - leadership;
   - drive, energy;
   - ability to communicate;
   - interpersonal skills.

Figure 12.2 continued overleaf

2. With a fast-changing environment there is an increased requirement for managers to:

   - look outwards to take in new trends and ideas;
   - optimise solutions from complex or conflicting data;
   - respond quickly;
   - cope under pressure.

3. Given the expectations of change over the next five years, successful managers will have highly developed:

   - ability to think then create action steps;
   - strategic capability;
   - communication skills;
   - curiosity.

4. Winning companies in the future will have built a competitive advantage from the skill, energy and commitment of its management and workers. Implications for successful managers are:

   - training programmes must match future needs;
   - management development and succession planning take a high priority;
   - personal development must receive more time.

5. Leadership is not easy to define yet it is an essential characteristic of a successful manager. Leadership qualities can be improved through practice. Successful leaders are:

   - flexible;
   - inspirational;
   - enthusiastic;
   - people-oriented;
   - able to build trust;
   - open;
   - of high integrity;
   - experimental;
   - able to communicate well;
   - ready to enable others to act.

6. Strategy is an essential building block for a business striving to maximise value. As successful strategy:

   - is based on appropriate internal and external analysis;
   - is based on core competences;
   - involves a broad spectrum of management;
   - is communicated appropriately and effectively.

Figure 12.2 Key messages for managers

A final thought

The key aim of this book is to stimulate the reader to think about how they can be more effective. How can each manager be more successful? I have not tried to offer a universal prescription of learning that will instantly create successful managers. No such universal panacea exists. However, we have covered a broad spectrum of subjects that I hope will have stimulated the reader to think about effectiveness both in their present role and in the future. The book has plenty of practical tips that have worked well in particular settings.

Real value from reading this book will only be obtained if the reader commits to an action plan, thoughtfully based, action-oriented and, as always, calculated to deliver shareholder value. This is best achieved through consistently high, improved personal performance. Go to it!

Appendix I General Management Questionnaire

About you

1. (a) Which age band do you come under?   ....   under 30

    31–40

    41–50

  ....   over 50

   (b) Do you have any formal business training, e.g. MBA, Advanced Business Programmes?

   (c) When were these courses undertaken in relation to your first general management post?

   (d) Was your first general management appointment within the organisation in which you were then working or in another outside company?

2. When you were appointed to your first general management position, what training did you receive? (e.g. company, reading, courses)

3. What were the first actions you took in that role? (e.g. learning, strategy, organisation, changes) Can you also give some idea of the time frame within which these actions took place?

About your views

1. What are the most important characteristics in a general manager
   (choose up to four)

	Put in priority order
Ability to communicate	. . . .
Drive, energy	. . . .
Intellectual capacity	. . . .
Interpersonal skills	. . . .
Knowledge of industry	. . . .
Leadership qualities	. . . .
Successful track record	. . . .
Others (specify)	. . . .

2. What is the best way to choose potential general managers?

3. Do you believe that formal training in general management is
   desirable as a precursor to the first appointment? If so, what would
   you recommend?

About your company

1. How do you identify potential general managers?

2. What training in general management skills do you provide? Do you
   provide this training prior to a new appointment?

3. What success factor have you had with newly appointed general
   managers in their first role who have come from different functions?

4. Is there any background that has a higher success rate than others? (e.g. sales, marketing, finance, production, technical etc.)

About your time

How much of your time do you devote to the following areas? (approximations only are needed)

Approx. %

Strategy
(creation and implementation) . . . .

Controlling
(meetings, performance, measuring) . . . .

Communication
(internal and external) . . . .

Maintaining relationships
(with customers, suppliers, government and
community) . . . .

Management Development
(top staff selection, succession planning, training,
education) . . . .

Personal Development . . . .

Others
(would you kindly specify main areas) . . . .

100%

Would you prefer your views to be anonymous or may I quote any of your comments?

Anonymous . . . .
May quote . . . .

Would you like a copy of the summary?   . . . .

                                                Yes   No

Name   . . . .

Company   . . . .

Address   . . . .

                     . . . .

Thank you very much for your help.

Appendix II Professionals' Questionnaire

Survey on general management

1. What is the best way to identify potential managers for their first assignment?

2. Are there any backgrounds that give a new general manager a better chance of success?

3. Rank in order *four* of the following as key characteristics in a general manager.

	Put in priority order
Ability to communicate	. . . .
Drive, energy	. . . .
Intellectual capacity	. . . .
Interpersonal skills	. . . .
Knowledge of industry	. . . .
Leadership qualities	. . . .
Successful track record	. . . .
Others (specify)	. . . .

4. Thinking about the next 5–10 years, would you change this list? Please explain why.

5. On average, how would you expect to see a successful general manager who is leading a company allocate his time?

	Approx. %
Strategy (creation and implementation)	. . . .
Controlling (meetings, performance measuring)	. . . .
Communication (internal and external)	. . . .
Maintaining relationships (with customers, suppliers, govt., community)	. . . .
Management development (top staff selection, succession planning, training, education)	. . . .
Personal development	. . . .
Others (kindly specify)	. . . .

Thank you for your help.

I would like a summary report   Yes . . . . .   No . . . . .

Name   . . . .
Address   . . . .
             . . . .
             . . . .
             . . . .

Glossary of Terms

Activity-based costing (ABC) A method of allocating all costs to activities in an organisation as distinct from cost centres. ABC focuses on where the costs came from rather than the traditional view of allocating overhead costs.

Activity-based management (ABM) An extension of ABC which provides management with information that is helpful to manage the business by associating costs with special activities. Examples would include true customer profitability – profitability by product groups.

Asset turn The ratio of sales to capital employed.

Balance sheet A statement of assets and liabilities of an enterprise or organisation at a particular date.

Biotechnology The use of biological materials and processes more frequent in the food industry and the health industry.

Book value The value of an asset as recorded in the company's books. This is often at historical cost by may also be at valuation.

Bottom line (of the profit and loss account) The residual profit (usually net profit before tax).

Business plan Sometimes called a strategic plan. This is a short document that describes the goals and how the business will get there, usually over a three to five year period.

Business Process Re-engineering (BPR) A method of examining business processes from first principles to remove those that do not add value thus significantly reducing costs or improving the service to customers.

Capex Capital expenditure.

Career development review The process to discuss with an employee his/her aspirations for progress in the organisation and to contrast this with opportunities seen by the employer. Training needs will flow from these discussions.

Career planning The planning of steps in an individual's career.

Chaos theory A body of thinking that suggests that in a fast-changing world the greatest imperative is to be reactive. Precedents and plans are of very limited use for current situations.

Corporate governance The rules and procedures put in place to see that a company is properly run.

Cost of capital The cost to the firm of servicing its total capital base including equity and debt.

Current asset An asset on the balance sheet which would normally be convertible into cash within a year.

Current liability A liability on the balance sheet that would normally be payable in a year.

Data processing Computing.

Debt/equity ratio (Sometimes called gearing). This is the proportion of a firm's assets financed by debt, as distinct from the equity.

Demographics The study of changing patterns of population according to age, sex or nationality.

Depreciation The amount provided for the diminution of an asset over the year. This is not a cash cost but is a charge against the profit and loss account.

Discounted cash flow (DCF) A technique usually used in capital project evaluation of adjusting future cash flows for the time value of money (called the discount rate). This then enables comparisons to be made over time.

Dividend load The number of times the dividend payment is covered by earnings after tax.

Earnings per share (eps) Tax paid profits before dividend distributions divided by the weighted average number of shares issued.

Earnings yield Earnings per share divided by the share price multiplied by 100 per cent.

Electronic data interchange (EDI) A paperless transfer of data between two compatible computer systems.

Electronic mail (E-Mail) Sending letters or documents via computer.

Gearing (see debt to equity ratio)

Interest cover The number of times the total interest payments are covered by profits before interest and tax.

Internal rate of return (IRR) The compound interest rate (usually after tax) that is earned from the future cash flows when compared with the initial investment.

Market value Generally used to indicate the total value of the company on the stock exchange at a particular time. It is calculated by multiplying the share price by the total number of shares in issue.

Mentoring Where a senior, experienced manager in an organisation guides and advises a younger, developing manager. The mentor is usually not the individual's direct boss.

Mission The major purpose for which the company exists.

Net present value The resultant sum when all future cash flows have been discounted by the appropriate rate. This discount rate is usually the rate required by the investor.

Operating cash flow (OCF) Operating profits plus non-cash items less capital expenditure plus or minus changes in working capital.

Operating profits (OP) Profits before interest and tax and before dividend distributions. (Sometimes also referred to as EBIT or earnings before income tax.)

Payback (payback period) The time it takes to repay the total original investment in cash terms and after all expenses.

Payout ratio Dividends as a percentage of the profits after tax.

Price/earnings ratio (P/E) The company's share price divided by the earnings per share. (The higher the ratio the more highly regarded the company.)

Profit Before Tax (PBT) Sometimes called the pre-tax profit. Profit after all expenses but before income tax.

Return on capital employed (ROCE) Operating profit divided by capital employed. It is also useful to understand that trading margin (OP to sales) multiplied by the asset turn will also yield the ROCE.

Shareholder value In a general sense, this focuses actions on improving the long-run net wealth of a company for the benefit of shareholders. Shareholder value is created if investments earn more than the cost of value or if executive decisions improve the shareholders' funds.

Share options Rights given (usually to employees) to buy shares in the future at a price fixed today.

Sourcing Procurement of supplies often from a third party.

Strategic alliance A co-operative agreement between two or more independent companies for a specific purpose, usually of a long-term nature, to achieve strategic objectives that would not be possible independently.

Strategic business unit (SBU)   A profit centre within a company.

Succession planning   The process of preparing succession for key executives in an organisation.

Supply chain   The relationship between customers, manufacturers, distributors and suppliers.

Synergy   The ability to derive greater benefits from a total than from the sum of the individual parts, for example, 'two and two will equal five'.

Value engineering   Analysis of the costs of raw materials and processes then comparing these costs with the benefits. This enables a judgement to be made whether costs can be taken out of the process without reducing customer value.

Working capital   Funding for short-term requirements of the business. Essentially, working capital is debtors plus stock minus creditors.

Zero-based budgeting   Budgeting without reference to historical levels of spend. A device to remove unnecessary costs by challenging the benefit of each major item of proposed expenditure.

References

Adair, John, *Great Leaders*, Talbot Adair Press, 1989.

Autry, J. A., *Love and Profit: The Art of Caring Leadership*, Morrow, 1991.

Baden-Fuller, Charles, and John Stopford, *Rejuvenating the Mature Business*, Routledge, 1992.

Beer, Michael, Russell A. Eisenstat and Bert Spector, 'Why Change Programmes Don't Produce Change', *Harvard Business Review*, Nov.–Dec. 1990.

Belbin, R. Meredith, *Management Teams: Why they Survive or Fail*, Heinemann, 1990.

Bennis, Warren, *On Becoming a Leader*, Hutchinson Business Books, 1990.

Benson, Herbert, with William Proctor, *Your Maximum Mind*, The Aquarius Press, 1988.

Booth, Rupert, *Control your Overheads*, Pitman, 1994.

Bowman, Lee, with Andrew Crofts, *High Impact Business Presentations: How to Speak like an Expert and Sound like a Statesman*, Business Books, 1991.

Cadbury, Sir Adrian, *The Company Chairman*, Director Books, Simon & Schuster International Group, 1990.

Chan, K. W., and A. Mauborgue Rennee, 'Parables of Leadership', *Harvard Business Review*, July–August, 1992.

Cokins, Gary, Alan Stratton and Jack Hebling, *An ABC Manager's Primer*, Irwin, 1993.

Daniels, John L., and N. Caroline Daniels, *Global Visions: Building New Models for the Corporation of the Future*, McGraw-Hill, 1993.

De Bono, Edward, *Lateral Thinking for Management*, Penguin Books, 1982.

De Bono, Edward, *Opportunities*, Penguin Books 1983.

De Bono, Edward, *Sur/Petition, Creating Value Monopolies when Everyone Else is Merely Competing*, Harper, 1992.

De Pree, Max, 'The Leadership Quest: Three Things Necessary', *Business Strategy Review*, Spring, 1993.

Demb, Ada, and F. Friedrick Neubauer, *The Corporate Board: Confronting the Paradoxes*, Oxford, 1992.

Drucker, Peter F., *Managing for the Future: The 1990s and Beyond*, Dutton 1992.

Drucker, Peter F., *The New Realities*, Heinemann, 1989.

Earl, Michael J., *Management Strategies for Information Technology*, Prentice-Hall, 1989.

Ernst & Young, *Biotechnology's Impact in Europe*, 1994 (note: an in-house publication).

Gabarro, John J., *The Dynamics of Taking Charge*, Harvard Business School Press, 1987.

Gabarro, John J. and K. P. Kotter, 'Managing your Boss', *Harvard Business Review*, January–February 1980.

Gross, Richard D., *Psychology, The Science of Mind and Behaviour*, Hodder & Stoughton, 1992, 2nd edn.

Hale, Sandra J. and Mary M. Williams, *Managing Change*, Urban Institute Press, 1989.

Hamel, Gary and C. K. Prahalad, *Competing for the Future*, Harvard Business School Press, 1994.

Hammer, Michael and James Champy, *Re-engineering the Corporation*, Brealy, 1993.

Handy, Charles, *The Age of Unreason*, Business Books Limited, 1989.

Handy, Charles, *The Empty Raincoat*, Hutchinson, 1994.

Haspelagh, Phillipe C. and David B. Jemison, *Managing Acquisitions: Creating Value through Corporate Renewal*, Free Press, 1991.

Hax, Arnoldo C. and Nicolas Majluf, *The Strategy Concept and Process: A Pragmatic Approach*, Prentice-Hall, 1991.

Hunt, John W., *Managing People at Work*, McGraw-Hill, 1992, 3rd edn.

IMD, 'Perspectives for Managers', No. 3, June 1994.

Kakabadse, Andrew W., *The Wealth Creators*, Kogan, 1991.

Kanter, Rosabeth Moss, *When Giants Learn to Dance: Mastering the Challenge of Strategy, Management and Careers in the 1990s*, Simon & Schuster, 1989.

Kanter, Rosabeth Moss, Barry A. Stein and Todd Jick, *The Challenge of Organisational Change, How Companies Experience It and Leaders Guide It*, The Free Press, 1992.

Katzenbach, Jon R. and Douglas K. Smith, *The Wisdom of Teams*, McKinsey, 1993.

Kay, John, *Foundations of Corporate Success: How Business Strategies Add Value*, Oxford University Press, 1990.

Koch, Richard, *The Financial Times Guide to Management and Finance: An A–Z of Tools, Terms and Techniques, Financial Times*, Pitman Publishing, 1994.

Kotter, John P., *A Force for Change*, Free Press, 1990.

Kotter, John P., *The General Managers*, Free Press, 1982.

Kotter, John P., *The Leadership Factor*, Free Press, New York, 1988.

Kotter, John P., 'What Leaders Really Do', *Harvard Business Review*, May–June, 1990.

Kotter, John P., and James Hesketh, *Corporate Culture and Performance*, Free Press, 1992.

Kouzes, James M., and Barry Z. Posner, *Credibility: How Leaders Gain and Love It, Why People Demand It*, Jossey Bass, 1993.

Lessem, Ronnie, and F. Fredrich Neubauer, *European Management Systems: Towards Unity out of Cultural Diversity*, McGraw Hill, 1994.

McCrae, Hamish, *The World in 2020*, Harper-Collins, 1994.

McTaggart, James M., Peter W. Kontes and Michael C. Mankins, *The Value Imperative*, The Free Press, 1994.

Morrison, Ann M., *The New Leaders*, Jossey-Bass, 1992.

Morton, Clive, *Becoming World Class*, Macmillan, 1994.

Naisbitt, John, *Megatrends*, Warner Books, 1982.

Obeng, Eddie and Stuart, Crainer, *Making Engineering Happen*, Pitman, 1994.

Pascale, Richard T., *Managing on the Edge*, Viking, 1990.

Pearson, Ian and Peter Cochrane, *200 Futures for 2020*, BT Laboratories, 1994.

Peters, Tom, *Liberation Management*, Macmillan, 1992.

Peters, Tom and Nancy Austin, *A Passion for Excellence: The Leadership Difference*, Collins, 1985.

Pfeffer, Jeffrey, *Managing with Power*, Harvard Business School Press, 1992.

Pfeffer, Jeffrey, *Competitive Advantage through People*, Harvard Business School Press, 1994.

Porter, Michael, *Competitive Strategy: Techniques for Analysing Industries and Competitors*, The Free Press, 1980.

Porter, Michael, *Competitive Advantage: Creating and Sustaining Superior Performance*, The Free Press, 1985.

Porter, Michael, *The Competitive Advantage of Nations*, Macmillan, 1990.

Prahalad, C. K., and Gary Hamel, 'The Core Competence of the Corporation', *Harvard Business Review*, 68, No 3, 1990.

Schwab, Klaus, (ed.) *Overcoming Indifference: 10 Key Challenges in Today's Changing World*, New York University Press, 1995.

Schwab, Klaus, and Claude Smadja, 'Power and Policy; The New Economic World Order', *Harvard Business Review*, November–December 1994.

Semler, Ricardo, 'Managing without Managers', *Harvard Business Review*, September–October, 1989.

Smith, Terry, *Accounting for Growth*, Century Business, 1992.

Tait, Ruth, *Roads to the Top*, Macmillan, 1995.

Toffler, Alvin, *Power Shift: Wealth and Violence at the Edge of the 21st Century*, Bantam, 1990.

Van Maurik, John, *Discovering the Leader in You*, McGraw-Hill, 1994.

Waterman, Robert H., *The Renewal Factor: Building and Maintaining your Company's Competitive Edge*, Bantam Press, 1988.

Index